Praise for Not Even Crabs Walk Backwards

Like a clear racing road map this book is your ultimate GPS to success!

–Lucas Di Grassi, former Formula 1 racing driver

This isn't just a book – it's a manual of knowledge, all wrapped up in bite-size chunks so you can start transforming your life today!

–Steve Mertz, international business lawyer

This book really shows you how much you are in control of your life and you didn't even notice and just by impressing the ideas written on it in to your subconscious mind your life already begins to change right in front of your eyes and you will notice!

–Susmita Bhattacharya, Indian classical and traditional singer

Not Even Crabs Walk Backwards – This book reinforces that 'positive thinking creates positive actions.' The key to success is being tenacious. 'Go for Gold' and you'll be a 'winner.'

–Paula Wyllie, general manager, Retail Design
Westfield Shoppingtowns Ltd

In a world of chaos that many people are living in, Jorge's Not Even Crabs Walk Backwards can make it very clear how to organize your thoughts.

Not Even Crabs Walk Backwards is truly a journey to the centre of the self. A lively, insightful read, with inspirational quotes from Shaw to Shakespeare. Jorge Gannuny has drawn from his extensive experience as a personal trainer to create a must read practical guide on how to flex and strengthen the mind.

This book is a good inspiration to get your power within, and start to savour the best in life! ... without procrastinating.

I have been training with Jorge for long time with great success ... if results are what you have been searching for, this is your chance!

In Not Even Crabs Walk Backwards, Jorge coaches you, very simply, how to take control of the cinema in your mind. The beauty of this book is in that you are the scriptwriter, the director and the actor of your own destiny! This is a very captivating and easy to read book that I recommend to all of you who are ready to explore the unlimited power within! Read it!

Not Even Crabs Walk Backwards hits you like a slap on the face! If things are not going right you definitely should look at some of the principles this book offers and put them into practice! Jorge, you have made us all think again!

Not Even Crabs Walk Backwards provides a clear and compelling explanation of how we learn to think and feel about ourselves and how we can take greater control over this process to achieve real, positive change in our lives.

Foreword by Bob Proctor – Featured in the movie *The Secret*

Not Even Crabs Walk Backwards

So Why Do You?

JORGE GANNUNY

CHILI PEPPER PUBLISHING

CHILI PEPPER PUBLISHING
50 Sinclair Road, London
W14 0NH, UK

E-mail:	admin@chilipepperpublishing.com
ISBN:	978 -1-5136-3640-5
Cover:	Daniela Savone
Text:	Eric Choi
Edit:	Jorge Gannuny

COMPANIES, ORGANIZATIONS, INSTITUTIONS, AND INDUSTRY PUBLICATIONS. Quantity discounts are available on bulk purchases of this book for reselling, educational purposes, subscription incentives, gifts, sponsorship, or fundraising. Special books or book excerpts can also be created to fit specific needs such as private labeling with your logo on the cover and a message from a VIP printed inside. For more information, please contact our Special Sales Department at Chili Pepper Publishing.

CAUTION:

THIS INFORMATION IS POWERFUL!

THE LIFE YOU WILL CREATE USING THIS KNOWLEDGE IS SO
RICH AND SATISFYING THAT YOU WILL NEVER AGAIN RETURN
TO THE PLACE YOU WERE BEFORE.

Dedication

This book is dedicated to all of you who were on the edge of quitting but heard a voice inside and decided to persevere and not give up. Your efforts will be rewarded.

And
To my mum and dad!

Acknowledgments

To Bob Proctor (www.bobproctor.com), who showed me the art of thinking and the power of my mind.

To the photographer Camilla Molnar, who worked on the back cover picture.

To the design team, who managed to create this incredible book cover.

To all of the team members of **Not Even Crabs Walk Backwards**, without you this project would not be possible.

To my dear friend Leesha Malik for lending me her beautiful home to produce the back cover photo.

My special thanks to my parents, Elias and Wilma Gannuny. Mum and Dad, I am where I am today because of your support and guidance. Thank you for always believing in me and letting me do everything that I wanted.

My best friend and brother Alexandre and my sister Iara for being there when I needed you most.

The late Ronnie Young, a true Scottish man who taught me the value of reading books.

My wife and best friend Sharona Gannuny for her support. Without you, lots of things would not be possible in my life.

My beautiful children, Brandon and Ayden.

And finally, thanks to the Universe for providing us with everything that we want and need when you know how to work with the laws.

Contents

Foreword, by Bob Proctor

For me everything started ove 50 years ago when I was given a book by Napoleon Hill (Think and Grow Rich), a book that I have been studying every day since.

Today I own a number of very prosperous companies that operate worldwide, which I built using the principles of Napoleon Hill.

Some books, when deeply studied, can really transform your life and the lives of people around you; Napoleon Hill's philosophy is a well of deep knowledge that explores the true nature and meaning of success. Any time I find a book that continues to expand on the truths of Think and Grow Rich, I am happy to recommend it to my friends and associates.

Not Even Crabs Walk Backwards is a book I am proud to read and pass on to others. Following in the giant footsteps of Hill, the author Jorge Gannuny provides self-improvement techniques and a process that can help individuals succeed.

Jorge uses real-life stories to reveal the hidden and often ignored creative power within us. It soon becomes apparent that each of us has the ability to take full control of our personal destinies. Not Even Crabs Walk Backwards is a very good read from the start to the end.

You will definitely unlock the key for having more fulfilled and harmonious relationships, financial security, satisfying careers, mustering bad habits, getting fit and enjoying good health.

When you start to read this book, you will see things really changing for you, and your awareness will increase. Jorge exposes us to the marvellous universal laws that can work in our favour 24 hours a day, when applied properly.

So prepare yourself, fasten your seat belt and enjoy the ride!

–Bob Proctor, international bestselling author of *You Were Born Rich*
and Chairman of Proctor and Gallagherin Stitute

Introduction

Did you like to go to the beach when you were a kid? I did. I was born by the sea, and Mum and Dad loved to take my brother and me to the beach every weekend to play. Mum even took us in the middle of the winter, to give you an idea of how much we liked going there. Isn't that strange how kids like to play with water? Why do kids like to jump in puddles no matter how well dressed they may be?

On one special occasion, Dad decided to take the whole family on a trip to a different seashore. I was astonished by the beauty of it. I was at this beautiful golden beach surrounded by crystal clear water. My brother and I decided that we were going to build sand castles. We were digging holes when suddenly we spotted a few white crabs coming out of the sand and going towards the ocean. I started to chase them, you know, as all little kids do when they get new toys to play with. I was quite desperate to grab one in my hands, but they were too fast for me. Unfortunately, at that time, I had no understanding of sprinters' techniques.

I spent the next few minutes looking at the crabs, trying to play with them, and I realised something quite strange; the little creatures walked only sideways or forwards. I was really excited by this, and I spent the whole afternoon imitating crabs, but I was walking backwards without even noticing that I was doing it wrongly. Crabs walk sideways and not backwards; my brother was laughing at me saying that I was crazy.

While running backwards, I caught the attention of my dad.

'Why are you walking backwards Jorge?' he asked.

'I am walking like crabs do,' I replied.

My dad sat me down and explained to me that I was a little boy, not a crab, and boys walk only forwards, not backwards. Then he pinpointed, 'Not even crabs walk backwards.'

I didn't understand this message when I was little, but now I live my life with this principle: 'Never walk backwards in life.' As human beings we have unlimited potential. We should focus on progressing, not regressing. Imagine what would happen if you drove your car looking only at the mirror; you would definitely crash, wouldn't you? That is why you should not worry about what happened, but rather focus on your present, and this will improve your future.

This is not a book of good ideas; this is a book of self-empowerment used by successful people. The principles in this book are nothing new; you probably have heard most of them before. The difference is that I put the information together in a way that it is easy to understand.

I met one of my first mentors through a book. I was 19 years old when I read Dr Joseph Murphy's The Power of Your Subconscious Mind (1962). After that I read hundreds of books, and still counting, on psychology, personal development, philosophy, quantum physics, religion. I attended seminars and workshops and listened to thousands of hours of audio programs (including tapes, which are now referred to as antiques). I took in a huge amount of information and began to explore what we truly are as human beings. After that, I had a better understanding of who I really am.

I began to think differently, and my results improved. I felt better about myself, and I did better in all areas of my life: finance, career, relationships, inner life. Basically, everything in my life was changing very quickly.

Now I have fun sharing with people how to have more successful and fulfilled experiences in different areas of their life.

In life, make sure that you never walk over anybody to become successful.

Chapter 1

Responsibility

You Can't Win Without This

You have so much more potential than you can even imagine. Petite women have lifted cars; rich people have given everything away to serve as missionaries; poor people have worked themselves out of the ghettos to become billionaires and uneducated farmers have solved world crisis. Anything is possible if you can persist and know how to get the most from yourself. You do that by taking 100 per cent responsibility for your life!

Put Yourself Totally on the Line Every Time

The first element in putting yourself totally on the line every time you do something is to be wholly committed to yourself and to your activity. Until you are committed, there is room for hesitancy, that chance to draw back from progress; the result is always one of ineffectiveness. Make a steadfast resolution to put behind your effort everything you have emotionally, mentally and physically, without hesitation; this is of critical importance. You must not let any fear of losing even enter your mind.

Failure does not exist! You may have some difficulty in rationalizing this concept, but all that is necessary is to view it from a different perspective than that with which you have been conditioned all your life.

There are NO failures, only lessons!

Therefore, regardless of the outcome of your efforts, you still gain experience. You may not attain exactly what you had previously expected, in precisely the manner you intended, but you do gain knowledge. You still come out a winner with success to build upon even further in the future.

Just remember never to be afraid to lose because in reality, you aren't really losing at all. As long as you never give less than your best effort, the absolute minimum you will gain is self-satisfaction in having done your best.

Many times we are afraid to take responsibility for our failures because failures oftentimes hurt. In our minds failing to achieve a goal shows weakness. As a society we have been wrongfully taught that failure is negative. Great achievers know that is not so. Thomas Edison tried 10,000 times before he discovered an electric light bulb that would work. While some would say he failed 10,000 times, Edison looked at it differently. He said that he had discovered 10,000 ways that light bulbs would not work.

A life spent making mistakes is not only more honourable but more useful than a life spent in doing nothing.

–George Bernard Shaw

Failure is the opportunity to begin again more intelligently.

–Henry Ford

At one time Babe Ruth, the Hall of Fame baseball player, held the record for the most home runs, 714. At the same time, he held the record for the greatest number of strikeouts, 1330. Do you think there might be a correlation? Of course. If you fail twice as much, you will generally succeed twice as much, as long as you don't quit. Incidentally, which of Babe Ruth's records do you think he is known best for, his home runs or his strikeouts?

In the event that you do not attain your original goal immediately, refuse to make excuses. Reaffirm your commitment to work longer and harder with a positive attitude and you will ultimately attain your goal. Even the great inventors and sportsman of the world failed. There is a right time and place for everything.

A sales achiever accepts the responsibility to make it happen, no matter what it takes. We can learn from babies who, when learning to walk, persist until they learn to walk.

When was the last time you heard about people who became so frustrated Learning to walk as children that they decided to crawl for the rest of their lives? Obviously, it doesn't happen, but some people have less sense than a baby. They approach a task with an 'I'll try' attitude.

The word **try** is really an invalid word. Let me give you an example. Try to pick up a chair. Grab hold of the chair and try to lift it. I said just try. Now, you are probably thinking, 'How do I carry out the act of trying without actually lifting the chair?' You see, you can't. In reality you either lift the chair or you don't. There is no such thing as trying to lift the chair. It's one or the other. Catch yourself the next time you hear that word come from your mouth. Either commit or don't. There is no in-between.

In the movie **Star Wars**, Yoda asked Luke Skywalker to commit (take responsibility) for winning the battle with the force of darkness, Darth Vader. Luke said, 'I will try.' Yoda responded with, 'Luke, either you do or do not; there is no try.'

Persist until you achieve your results, and believe that the world is on your side because it is. Don't allow fear of failure to immobilize you. Fear is a movement of your mind which creates what you expect.

*What you fear, you will attract, and what you experience
is what you expect.*

We can put fear of failure behind us by doing the things we fear. Do the things you fear, and you will control fear! By refusing to back down, refusing to quit and persisting in achieving your results, you will succeed.

When you are feeling down and ready to quit, step back and take another look at your situation for a moment; view it from the point of a challenge. What you are attempting may not be that conventional, but you must challenge the conventional in order to succeed. You need the perseverance to do as you dream because you are betting on yourself. You must have an unreasonable passion – virtually an obsession – for being your best. After all, an obsession is a persistent, disturbing preoccupation with an often unreasonable idea. Break away from convention and you will be amazed at how you will always attract all the help you need.

Never Turn Against Yourself During Tough Times

The reality of life is that things don't always go perfectly for all of us, all the time; accomplishing our goals can entail a lot of hard work and difficulties. That's what being human is all about, and it's perfectly normal.

The important thing is never to put yourself down in such situations and to maintain and reinforce a strong, positive attitude. To persevere is one of the most important principles. If you persevere, you will eventually get yourself back on the right track. If you use up your energy fighting yourself, you won't have any left to battle your opponent. That opponent may be anything from a particular person (sport) to a situation (other areas of life).

Your Mental Attitude Makes All the Difference

No athlete expects to enter a competition without first having spent considerable time and energy in practice. The same applies to whatever you want to do in attaining your goal. Contrary to common belief, practice should encompass about 10 per cent physical effort and 90 per cent mental preparation. Do whatever is necessary to get your mind focused. Practice with the same intensity and emotional commitment that you'll generate in the real situation.

Being mentally prepared helps accomplish numerous things simultaneously. It not only contributes to the building of positive accomplishment but also helps overcome the obstacles you will no doubt encounter along the road to success. To develop a never-ending list of affirmations which you can implement immediately, whenever necessary, it helps to be aware of some typical limiting statements in advance of your being faced with them. How often, in the process of attaining your goal, have you been bombarded with some of the following comments?

- You can't always have a job you can enjoy.
- You're dreaming; get real.
- Don't expect what you know you can't have.
- You don't know how to do that.
- You don't have enough education.
- You don't have sufficient experience.
- You aren't smart enough to do that.
- Sure, I'll believe that when I see it.
- Just who do you think you are anyhow?

Keep Your Perspective

When getting the most from yourself starts producing incredible, positive results, it is all too easy to be so immersed in all the detailed activity that you lose sight of the overall picture. Participating with that sort of intensity is an absolute necessity for success.

However, you must occasionally take on the role of a spectator for a moment, step outside this fervour of activity and look at yourself. This process will give you a brief break in the intensity, permit you to recharge your batteries with ever-expanding energy and enable you to re-enter the process more intensely. The process of retaining perspective on your activities is a very powerful tool for managing stress and maintaining emotional balance.

You can implement a number of proven methods to accomplish this stepping-out process. Combining them in different ways simultaneously can have an even greater positive impact.

Exercise

Take time each day to exercise both your body and mind. Go for a walk once a day. Purchase some exercise equipment to use at home. If you prefer, join a health club and participate in some aerobic and muscle exercising activities. Exercising helps to relieve stress as well as keeping you in shape physically. When you are stress free and healthy, you feel better about yourself, and the way you feel about yourself affects your performance.

React

Try to avoid the temptation to become a couch potato if you are prone to such enticement. Find something other than your job to work on that you enjoy doing: arts and crafts or a hobby. Where exercise strengthens the body, creativity strengthens the mind and can be a welcome release for those of us who don't have creative jobs. The change in mental or physical stimulation can be unbelievably positive and inspiring. Get those creative juices flowing in your mind; after all, the more you work your mind, the stronger it becomes.

Build Relationships

Take some time out on a regular basis to communicate effectively with a close friend, your spouse, your children, a relative or mentor. Discuss your current activity and goal, and use this person as a sounding board to help verify how well you are maintaining your perspective.

Seek Solitude

Being alone helps you collect your thoughts and relax. The human body can stay active only for so long before it needs to re-energize. Sometimes just watching a movie or reading a book can help you feel better and rejuvenate. Without proper rest you won't have the energy to accomplish all the tasks necessary to achieve your goal.

The credit belongs to the man
who is actually in the arena,
whose face is marred
by dust, sweat, and blood.
Who strives valiantly, who attempts,
and comes short, again and again,
who knows the great enthusiasm,
the greater devotion
and spends himself in a worthy cause,
who at the best
knows the triumph of high achievement
and at the worst, if he fails,
at least knows he failed daring greatly,
so that his place shall never be
with those cold and timid souls
who know neither victory nor defeat.

–General Douglas MacArthur

Chapter 2

How the Mind Works

Master or Servant

Every one of us thinks in pictures. When asked to think about the home where you were raised, a picture of that place should form in your mind. If I ask about your bedroom, you see a mental picture of your bedroom. Now, if I ask you to visualize a dog, you are able to conjure up an image of a dog; you don't think of an elephant or a snake. No matter where you are in the world, you could build some semblance of a dog, no matter what you have for material because you hold the image of that dog in your mind.

Are you capable of describing what your mind looks like? Many will imagine an image of a brain, a brain that may be incredibly messy and disorganised, but a brain nonetheless. In reality, your mind is not your brain. Your mind is an activity and shows itself in every aspect of your appearance and your life. If you want to take full responsibility for your life and actions, you must always carry a clear picture of your mind.

In 1934 Dr Thurman Fleet, a chiropractor and founder of the concept therapy movement, was very involved in the healing arts and thought we were approaching things in the wrong way. He said, 'All we are doing is treating the body. We are treating the symptoms, not the cause of the problem.' In our society we treat the physical aspect of the problem, not the cause. We take a pill that dulls the pain for a while only to have it return in eight hours. The way our medical system is designed, doctors do not have time to go into all of your belief systems. There is a saying: 'Out of sight, out of mind.' This is terribly un-true. Just because you are unable to feel the pain anymore doesn't mean the problem has gone away.

For example, I want you to imagine that your house has caught fire and your smoke alarm goes off. You walk over to the storage closet and find a hammer and proceed to smash the smoke alarm until it stops beeping. You return the hammer and sit on the couch to watch television. You wouldn't even consider doing this. Why do we do it in our body? Pain or disease is our body's innate wisdom telling us there is something wrong in the core of our body. We are not synchronized.

What we think determines what happens to us, so if we
want to change our lives, we need to stretch our minds.

–Wayne Dyer

The Stick Person

Fleet understood this. He drew a very simple picture to represent the mind, but it is one of the most important pictures to understand. His idea is called the Stick Person, and you cannot hear about this enough. Understanding the Stick Person picture could save your life, as it has already done with many others around the world. This picture brings order and understanding to your mind. I am now going to show you how the Stick Person works.

A helpful tool, the Stick Person explains how thoughts affect how you see yourself. This tool will also help you to see how your thoughts manifest concrete things in your exterior world.

Fleet developed a drawing in which the head is much larger than the body is. This illustrates that our mind is dominant over the body and not the other way around, as many believe.

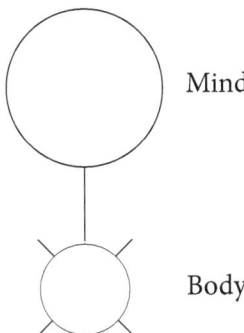

Mind

Body

Most of us focus all our conscious attention on the physical body and physical results without realizing that everything we experience in our body is an expression of our mind. Since your mind is an activity and it is not your physical brain, it is important to have a clear picture of what your mind looks like.

Using Fleet's idea of the Stick Person, we will split our minds into two parts: the conscious mind and the subconscious mind. We use our conscious mind for thinking; it is where we can accept, reject or neglect any idea which comes into it, but we use only a small percentage of our conscious mind.

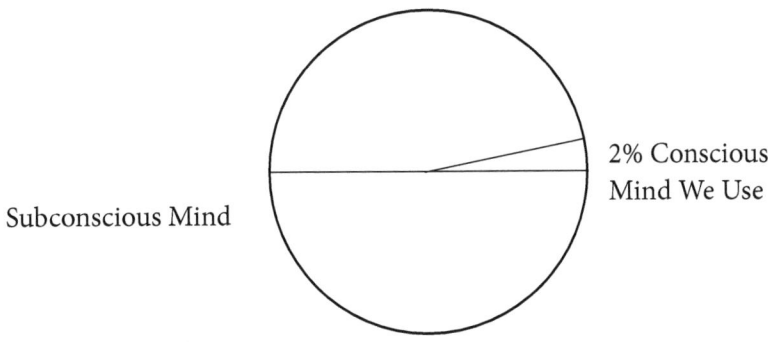

Subconscious Mind

2% Conscious
Mind We Use

Shakespeare, one of history's most prolific and profound creative writers, and certainly an artist extraordinaire wrote about the processes of the mind:

> *But then begins the journey in my head*
> *To work my mind, when body's work's expir'd;*
> *For then my thoughts – from far where I abide –*
> *Intend a zealous pilgrimage to thee,*
> *And keep my drooping eyelids open wide.*

–William Shakespeare

Our habits and belief systems are also formed in our subconscious mind. The subconscious mind is easily manipulated and is unable to reject an idea. It believes everything presented is truth. Think of people who act under the spell of hypnosis and how they wilfully do anything the hypnotists asks of them. The behaviours the subjects display are due to the fact they are acting through their subconscious mind; they are behaviours not normal to that person's everyday personality, as they have no ability during hypnosis to consciously think of the actions they display.

Following are some examples on how your subconscious mind affects your senses, which, in turn, affect your physical body.

Have you ever seen a landscape, painting or any visual that has moved you emotionally? You may see a picture of starving children and experience a feeling of anger and sadness that may move you to tears or make you shake with rage. A landscape may be so beautiful that you cannot verbally describe what you are seeing because the sight is just too much to put into words.

What about smell? Has the smell of freshly cooked food made your stomach growl when you had no clue you were hungry? There are also smells that have probably made you gag or cover your nose in disgust.

You can close your eyes and listen to a piece of music and be moved the same as seeing a beautiful work of art. Some musicians even say that they can see colours when they play music.

Why doesn't everyone agree on which foods taste delicious and which don't? You know what you like. You may love olives while someone genetically close to you despises them.

Your subconscious is unique to you and can evolve when it needs to. Ray Charles was a famous and very talented musician. Charles was born able to see, but as a young boy he lost his vision. At first his blindness crippled him, but, as the years went on, his hearing became extraordinary. Charles's mind had shifted its visual energies to hearing. It is said that he could hear a fly from across the room and could even tell when someone was coming before those with perfect sight had a clue. The mind is a powerful tool that can be rearranged to help you succeed in life.

What we think, feel or do forms the basis of our experience. Our memories are also stored in the subconscious. Old habits are hard to break because our self-image is made up of memories, and our old memories are emotionally connected to the past. The subconscious mind is the sum total of our experiences.

The subconscious mind stores experiences in the form of subtle impressions. Our tendencies form when these impressions interact and, depending on the tendencies, are likely to react in a certain way to a certain stimulus or situation. Our character is thus determined by the result of these tendencies. The subconscious is what allows us to know and do things instinctively. The subconscious mind never stops; it works while we sleep and throughout our whole day. Just as our body breaths and keeps its blood flowing involuntarily, so it keeps our mind ticking like a never-ending clock.

I'm sure the first time you drove a car you experienced sensory overload: the sight and sound of cars rushing past, the feel of the steering wheel's vibrations in your sweaty palms. You had to do everything in your power to drive that car. But now, truthfully, how many times have you 'spaced out' at the wheel? How many times have you thought about what you needed to accomplish that day or planned imaginary trips to some far off location while in transit? People say that you can't teach an old dog new tricks. False. Most people learn to drive at age 15 or 16, but many others learn far later. This just proves that your mind can be moulded and is constantly willing to change and learn new habits, for better or worse.

We know from neuroscience that thought produces chemical reactions in our brain which affect our physical body by changing the way we feel. We express through our actions what we feel, and what we feel is determined by our beliefs in our subconscious (emotional) mind. Our actions give us our results. Look at your results to see what you are thinking subconsciously. If you dislike the way your life is going, if the results you get daily are not what you want, you simply need to change the way you are thinking. Most people look at their results as their potential. This is entirely false. All the results we have ever obtained are due to the reflection of our past thoughts. When bad things occur in our lives, it is because we think of bad experiences and believe we will fail. Once we learn how to construct beautiful positive images in our minds, our results will reflect and our lives will benefit. Here is how.

What we call a mind is nothing but a heap or collection of different perceptions, united together by certain relations and supposed, though falsely, to be endowed with a perfect simplicity and identity.

–David Hume

We all have our conscious mind which is our thinking mind. The conscious mind makes the decisions. It has the ability to accept, reject or neglect an idea. Our environment also influences our actions every day through our five senses: that which we see, taste, hear, touch and smell. Our conscious mind obtains information through our five senses. In the womb and as a small child, either we had no conscious mind or it was underdeveloped. Our environment and what people say have a strong influence on what we believe as a child. Most of the occurrences that take place around us at this age are interpreted innocently and incorrectly. These interpretations have become our life belief systems.

You may have been raised to think you could never attend university because no one in your family ever went or that you had to attend university, or a certain university, because everyone in your family did. If these ideas were constantly put into your head at a young age, they will be as much a part of you as the language you speak. If you weren't born in an English-speaking country, you would speak a different language and have different beliefs. With this in mind, you need to realize that your beliefs are ingrained into your personality, but you do have the ability, through hard work, to change them.

> *There are two levels to your pain: the pain that you create now and the pain from the past that still lives on in your mind and body.*
>
> **–Eckhart Tolle**

The second part of our mind is, as discussed previously, our subconscious mind, which is our emotional centre. This is where our misinterpreted belief systems go. It is gullible and will believe whatever we tell it. It has to accept the pictures we give it. This part of the mind is like a mirror, but at the moment a wobbly carnival mirror. The imperfections in the mirror are morphed like our belief system. They alter the way we view ourselves and others around us. We may believe that we are not good looking enough, strong enough, thin enough, smart enough or qualified enough. This is the tree where we store our negative self-images, like a squirrel hiding nuts for winter. We all have quite a number of negative images. The curves and imperfections which distort our self-image were moulded into our mirror, the subconscious mind, when we were too young to prevent the occurrence. By changing our pictures to beautiful ones, we now change the outcome of our life's journey. The more we become aware, the more freedom we have in our life.

> *As long as the mind is enslaved, the body can never be free. Psychological freedom, a firm sense of self-esteem, is the most powerful weapon against the long night of physical slavery.*
>
> **–Martin Luther King, Jr.**

Imagine a prison. What do you see? A small cell with giant iron bars separating a criminal from freedom? Maybe a whole prison facility detaining all those who have failed to follow the laws of our society? In whatever case you probably don't see an image of yourself, but many of us are prisoners of our own minds, prisoners of our thoughts and what we think about is what we become, as Napoleon Hill stated. Most of the problems and dead ends we find ourselves in occur because of the prisons we have created in our subconscious mind from the erroneous belief systems we harbour.

Think what happens to you if you are angry or hurt by someone. First, you get the picture of that person or incident. That picture creates feelings, which show in your body. Your breathing may become fast and erratic. Your blood pressure may rise. You may start shaking. You may be so angry that you lose your focus. You became so riled up that you may forget what you want to say. The attack on your subconscious caused all these physical effects on your body, all because of a personal belief system. For example, I'm not good enough; I'm not pretty enough; I'm not smart enough. If we become aware of these beliefs, we can iron out the imperfections in our subconscious mind, take control of our goals and lead the lives we have always dreamed. Our journey becomes a journey worth taking.

The subconscious mind is your power centre. Everything you choose to enter in your subconscious must be positive, as it will become part of your subconscious. Your subconscious has no ability to reject. This part of us operates in an orderly manner. It expresses itself through you in feelings and actions. Any thought you consistently put into your subconscious will become a part of your personality and, in effect, part of your physical and mental health. Fixed ideas will then continue to express themselves without conscious assistance until they are replaced. These are your habits.

Do you still need to think about how to tie your shoe? When you sit for dinner, do you strain to use your silverware? No. When you were young, you did though. You had to learn all these actions at one point in your life. With practice and repetition, you can change anything you want. The subconscious mind is the God-like part of you referred to as spirit. It has no limits.

Your body is your home, the tool that accomplishes the tasks of the mind. The thoughts and images you construct in the mind are built in your body, for example: fear of a disease, worry, being happy with your life. Impressing a thought upon your subconscious mind (which is every cell of your body) moves your body to action. These actions you are involved in determine your results.

Thought + Feeling + Action = Results

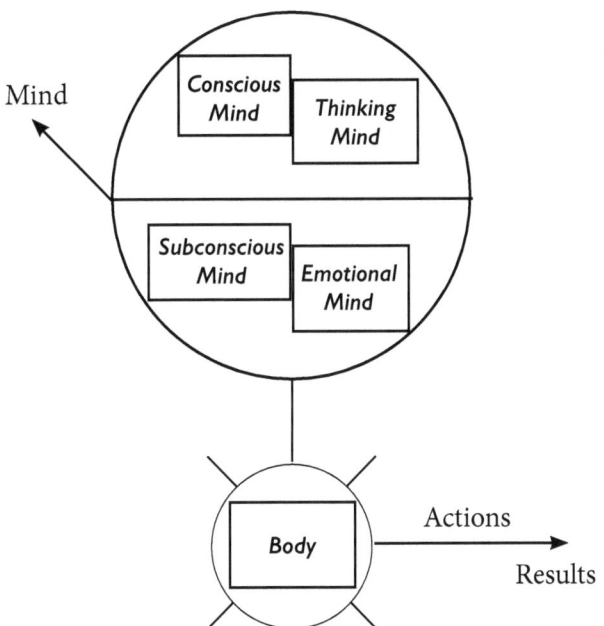

What does that mean? To change results, change your thoughts, which alter your feelings and move to actions. You can change the way you think, but you must know that it isn't easy. As with everything worth doing in this world, it will take dedication and perseverance. It may feel that you are fighting an uphill battle, and that is because you are. You are going against everything you were taught to believe. But just like driving a car or tying your shoes, the more you do it the easier it becomes. Hang in there and give it your all. Be the master, not the servant!

The mind is its own place, and in itself
Can make a Heaven of Hell, a Hell of Heaven.

–John Milton

Chapter 3

Knowledge Is Your Secret Weapon

*In times of change, learners inherit the earth, while the
learned find themselves beautifully equipped to deal with
a world that no longer exists.*

–Eric Hoffer

Contrary to popular belief, there is no such thing as an educated person. You are either learning or you are not. In today's world it is vitally important that you see the truth in Eric Hoffer's statement. The win or loss, which is waiting in the wings for every person, is enormous. You get to choose which you will experience.

Examine what Hoffer said. There are two obvious parts to his statement, and I will break them down to show you what they both mean and how it should inspire you to always move forwards and not stand still. The first part is very clear; how well it is understood is another subject.

'The learners will inherit the earth.'

It would probably be wise to look at the second part of his advice first. Then, if you happen to fall into the category Hoffer referred to, you can change your situation and win. 'The learned find themselves beautifully equipped to deal with a world that no longer exists.'

The world is constantly changing. Those unable to adapt to changes are as good as dead. Hoffer's statement shows this precisely.

In virtually every country of the world, you can find individuals, thousands of them, walking the streets with degrees in their hands, degrees from prestigious universities. They cannot find work. Why? These individuals view the conditions and circumstances that surround them as very frightening. They are the people whom Hoffer referred to as 'beautifully equipped to deal with a world that no longer exists.'

Let's look at the phrase **a world that no longer exists**. Every time the second hand ticks, the second before it belongs to the world that no longer exists. It becomes part of the past. The learned are carrying degrees that represent their knowledge of the past. The world that business cares about is the world in front of the second hand: the future.

Look around; the world is always changing and will never be the same again. Power is shifting, disappearing from some circles and reappearing in others. Some countries, companies and individuals who have held the power in the past are quickly losing it if, in fact, they have not already watched it melt in their hands. Their often smug, sometimes selfish, domineering, complacent attitude has cost them dearly. They are confused, and this confusion is frequently fuelled by their own ignorance. When that happens, it ultimately leads to anger or resentment, sometimes both. This negative energy is then quite frequently misdirected, possibly at their loved ones, which then causes an entirely new set of problems.

These people are clutched by an un-seen enemy, and their frustration is endless because they are not sure what has happened or what is happening. Their world seems to be turning upside down.

The learned that walk the streets unwilling to adapt to these changes belong to the past, not the future.

Businesses know this; they know that to survive in today's ever-changing environment one must be able to adapt and think on one's feet. The world is moving at such a high speed. Never before have such rapid changes occurred in a society. We went from the first gasoline automobile to the moon in less than a century, and we haven't slowed down yet. Yet there are still many communities with people who live in the past. They are living the lives taught to them by their parents and their grandparents before them. It confuses them that they are unable to get ahead, but this is because they don't realize they are looking behind. To get ahead one must constantly look forward. You would never try to climb a mountain by only looking at its base. Why then would you try to accomplish your goals by looking to the past?

The Romantic poets believed that to be relevant they had to rid themselves of the past and focus on the moment, or the present. This meant stepping away from the influences of historical figures and literature and learning from surroundings and local environments. If the Romantic poets had focused on only the past, they knew they could never become any better than their influences. Companies today are thinking in the same way. They have to survive. They are not looking for the ideas or people stuck in the past; they are looking for the person learning from the present and gazing into the future.

In the past individuals were recognized and rewarded for what they knew. Corporations waited on the sidelines dangling monetary rewards attempting to attract the graduates from the big-name universities of the world. They were the multi-million dollar MBA (which still has its qualities) management development programmers that corporations placed hope in for years. Almost everyone was conditioned to deify the intellect. Individuals were not properly recognized and rewarded for what they did.

Today the whole dynamic of how we communicate, inside and outside the office, is changing. The world is moving from an intellectual to a spiritual vibration. The majority of the population is still living with the old rules. People in every community have worked hard and disciplined themselves, based on what has worked in the past. They are doing what they were taught by their parents, teachers and employers. Unfortunately, they too are working with the old rules.

To succeed today a different approach is necessary. Step one is to learn from our mistakes. The world we live in is changing, always. We live in the new era. This is a spiritual world governed by exact universal laws. Everyone who studies these laws and incorporates them into every aspect of life will be richly rewarded. For instance, many successful companies have learned to value individuality and creativity on all levels, not just at the management level. I believe we would be wise to go back to the promise Hoffer shared with us in the first parts of his statement: 'In times of change, the learners inherit the earth.'

The learners are continually preparing themselves to adapt to the changes. Rather than reacting they are responding to these changes and responding appropriately. The learners are excited with the prospects of what this paradigm shift is bringing.

> *Great things are not done by impulse, but by a series of small things brought together.*
>
> **–Vincent Van Gogh**

Learn new small things every day. They will quickly add up to something great. You will see that great things aren't done all at once but over time, and one day you will step back and see all the amazing things you have done.

'Greatness is developed by doing little things in a great way, every day.' In 1903 Wallace D. Wattles shared that wisdom with us in a book he wrote on greatness. I agree with Wattles. I also believe it helps if you are exposed to great teachers along the way.

> *It pays to know how to purchase knowledge.*
>
> **–Napoleon Hill**

Five Great Thinkers

Over the past 20 years, I have been truly blessed. When it comes to teachers, I have had the best. It would be difficult to name them all and talk about all their qualities. There are, however, five people who have had a profound impact on my life. These individuals were, by any definition, great teachers. They possessed a deep understanding of the human personality and through their life's work developed the ability to clearly communicate the beautiful truths that they so clearly understood. To my good fortune, these great individuals instilled in me a love for learning.

James Allen, author of As a Man Thinketh: I have learnt very important lessons from James Allen. His book As a Man Thinketh, although a small book, has transmitted to me such a powerful message. I have learnt how powerful my thoughts are. He has taught me the lesson of calmness of the mind and purity of thoughts.

Dr Joseph Murphy, prosperity writer: Dr Joseph Murphy was one of my first mentors. I was only 19 when I discovered his work, not realizing how much influence he would have on me at a later stage. I learnt the power of positive thinking from Murphy. Although this part has been very hard to learn, I could not imagine my life without his material.

Dr Joe Vitale, 'the father of hypnotic marketing': Dr Joe Vitale has shown me how much the universe can bring us and how powerful it is to connect ourselves with the universe. I love his audio programmes, and each time I listen to them, I can feel the energy and flood of ideas coming to me.

Oprah Winfrey, champion of equality: Oprah Winfrey has been a mentor not only to me but also to millions of people around the world. She has taught me never to underestimate anyone and to respect men and women equally from any background, religion or culture, as we all have unlimited potentials.

Bob Proctor, leader in the human-potential movement: I met Bob Proctor at a point in my life where I wanted to empower myself and to go one step further than I could possibly imagine. For me Proctor is definitely the greatest thinker of our time. He taught me the art of thinking and how the mind works. Once I met Proctor, my life took a quantum leap. Ever since, I have started to enjoy the journey rather than focus just on the destination.

Laws of Learning

You are a spiritual being living in a physical body. You have been blessed with intellectual factors which, when properly utilized, give you awesome power. You have infinite potential. There is no limit to what you are capable of doing. All things are possible.

It is easy to become enthusiastic in today's world. The opportunities that surround you and me are so exciting and so vast in number that our real problem seems to be deciding which of the opportunities we will be involved with first. I have been fortunate enough to share this wonderful information all over the world for years. I cannot point to one instance where corporations or individuals have not compounded their effectiveness when they became totally immersed in learning how to live by universal law.

Laws are the unseen forces that govern everything on this earth and the entire universe. We cannot see the law of gravity, but we all live by it and can see its effect. A comprehension of physical laws is called physics. All mechanical devices operate according to precise and constant laws.

We have the technology to fly an aeroplane through the air at 30,000 feet because we are aware of the laws that make this possible. The laws have never changed, but now we are aware of them and can harness them to our advantage.

The best definition of natural law seems to be 'the uniform and orderly method of the omnipotent God (unlimited power of the Universe).'

As Wallace Wattles points out, in the original writing of his book The Science of Getting Rich, 'You can act in accordance with these laws or you can disregard them but you can in no way alter them. The laws forever operate and hold you to strict accountability and there is not the slightest allowance for ignorance… once a person learns and obeys these laws.'

Knowing that laws are absolute, Wattles states: 'There is a science of getting rich and it is an exact science, like algebra or arithmetic. There are certain laws, which govern the process of acquiring riches and once these laws are learned and obeyed by anyone, that person will get rich with mathematical certainty.'

Rich means having all forms of wealth: life, health, loving relationships, healthy and safe environment, financial prosperity, meaningful satisfying vocations and plenty of free time to enjoy the many gifts God has provided for us to access and wisely enjoy.

I am now going to share some of these universal laws with you.

Law of Vibration and Attraction

Everything in the universe vibrates; nothing rests. We really do live in an ocean of motion. This truly contains the great secret of life. You are always moving towards something, and it is always moving towards you; it is action and attraction. This is where your intuitive factor is used (or should be). You can use it to pick up other people's vibrations. When you consciously become aware of vibrations, you call them feelings. When you feel bad, you can change your feeling by thinking good thoughts. When you pick up a bad feeling from another person, you know that person must be thinking disturbing thoughts. You must not let those negative vibrations affect your way of thinking.

Your thoughts are vibrations that you send into the universe. When you concentrate, the vibrations are stronger. Your thoughts are cosmic waves of energy that penetrate all time and space (vibrations). Thought is the most potent vibration. You should always be delighted with yourself. All creation begins in thought. Your thought controls the vibration your physical body is in. Disease (DIS-EASE) is a body not at ease. Health is a body at ease.

Law of Perpetual Transmutation

This law tells us that energy is always moving, transmuting and changing. It takes one form and then another; but it never stands still. Everything we see, hear, taste, touch and smell is in constant change. Everything is energy, and energy is motion. So even things that appear completely solid and stable, such as a building or a piece of furniture, if you put samples of these substances under the microscope, you can actually see that they are changing in different forms right before your eyes.

The simplest example is water and the many forms it can take. In a solid state, it takes the form of ice, but when energy is added to the ice, heating it up, water goes from a solid to a liquid form. With even greater energy, liquid water turns into a gas and vaporizes.

Since most of us understand water, it is a good example. But everything in the world acts just like water. With the right kind of energy, anything can be changed.

Law of Relativity

Put your hand on a hot stove for a minute and it seems like an hour. Sit with a pretty girl for an hour and it seems like a minute. THAT'S relativity.

–Albert Einstein

You don't need to understand the whole of Einstein's theory of relativity! You just need to understand its metaphysical implication. There is no big nor small, fast nor slow, except by comparison. An understanding of this law will give you the means of solving the secrets of nature that seem paradoxical. The much discussed fourth dimension is nothing more or less than the dimension of vibration. Again, all rates of vibration are either high or low only by comparison with those above or below them. Whenever the law is properly used, you win. Let's remember that everyone does something better than you do, and, likewise, you do something better than every person you meet.

Say you play golf on the weekends. Relative to Tiger Woods you won't look like a good golfer, but compared to someone who has never picked up a club, you will look like a great golfer. If you are a chef by trade you would be a better cook than Tiger Woods.

Law of Polarity

Everything in the universe has its opposite. There would be no inside to a room without an outside. For example, if you referred to this side of the sheet of paper that these words are written on as the top, then the other side would be the bottom. You have a right and a left side to your body, a front and back. Every up has a down; every down has an up. The law of polarity not only states that everything has an opposite... it is equal and opposite. If it is three feet from the floor to the table, it is three feet from the table to the floor. If it is 212 miles from Paris to London, by law it must be 212 miles from London to Paris; it could not be any other way.

If something you considered bad happened in your life, then there has to be something good about it. If it was only a little bad, when you mentally work your way around to the other side, you will find it will be only a little good.

If you were walking up a flight of stairs and noticed that you were really out of breath, you may think, 'I should really start working out and eating right. I'm really out of shape.' You may not change your ways though. Being a little out of breath isn't the end of the world.

But if you suddenly had a heart attack, and the doctor told you lack of exercise and a terrible diet had caused the attack, you would probably immediately change your life style. The latter depends on the extremity of the former.

Law of Rhythm

The Law of Rhythm embodies the truth that is moving to and fro, flowing in and out, swinging backwards and forwards. There is a high tide and a low tide. Everything is flowing, both in and out, in accordance with the law. There is always a reaction to every action. Something must advance when something retreats; something must rise when something sinks. This law governs the movements of the planets in their orbits, and men and women can observe this law in their mental, physical and emotional states. The law of rhythm is universal. This can be observed in the rising and setting of the sun and the moon, the ebb and flow of tides, the coming and going of the seasons and the rhythmic swing of consciousness and unconsciousness.

You are not going to feel good all the time; no one does. If you did, you wouldn't even know it. The low feelings permit you to enjoy the high feelings.

Everything in the universe moves in cycles. The way the earth circles the sun makes the seasons. The seasons determine mating seasons and births. With every death something is born.

Think of the snowflake that falls on top of a mountain. It sits there in the wintertime until it is heated by the energy of the sun. Slowly it trickles down the mountainside until it flows into a creek. This creek flows until it merges with a river. The river rolls across the country merging with other rivers until finally it empties that snowflake into a giant ocean. That same flake may evaporate and rain down upon the ocean many times, but eventually it will rise into a cloud and move back inland. Forced up by the mountain, the water in the cloud will freeze and fall back as snow, and the cycle will continue for eternity. Everything returns to where it originated.

There will always be highs and lows in life. Reason gives us the ability to choose our thoughts (that is free will). Even when you are on a normal downswing, you can choose good thoughts with your free will and continue to move up towards your goal.

Law of Cause and Effect

Every cause has its effect; every effect, its cause. There is no such thing as chance. Everything happens according to law. Nothing in the entire universe ever happens unless it occurs according to law. Nothing ever escapes the law. It is impossible for the human mind to conceive of starting a new chain of causation for the simple reason that every effect must have a cause; and, in turn, that cause must have an effect. Thus we have the perpetual, never-ending cycle of cause and effect.

Ralph Waldo Emerson called the law of cause and effect the law of laws. You are, of course, very interested in results: your physical health, your relationships, the respect you earn and your material income. You must concentrate on the cause; the effect will automatically take care of itself. That is how the law works.

Law of Gender

This law governs what we know as creation. The word **creation** is often erroneously used, for, in reality, nothing is really created. All new things merely result from the changing of something that was into something else that now is. A giant redwood can be more than 2,000 years old. Once this enormous majestic being was a tiny seed. Over thousands of years, the seed grew into the tree. One day a gust of wind or a forest fire or some other cause will fall the tree. After it has fallen, the forest floor will quickly decompose the once king of the woods, and fungus, grasses, bushes and other trees will sprout from the energy it reinstates into the environment. The once giant redwood is now part of many other things. Its parts are now just spread throughout nature.

This law closes the cycle. This is the truth, the creative law. Male and female, yin and yang must unite for creation to take place.

This law also decrees that all seeds (ideas are spiritual seeds) have a gestation or incubation period before they manifest. In other words, when you choose a goal or build the image in your mind, a definite period must elapse before the image manifests in physical results. For example, a baby takes nine months. Plants, trees, flowers and corn all have their respective gestation period.

Chapter 4

Wasting Your Future

How to Overcome the Disease of Putting Things Off

The Procrastinator's Creed: I believe that if anything is worth doing, it would have been done already.

Procrastination

> \Pro*cras`ti*na'tion\, n. The act or habit of putting off doing something, especially out of habitual carelessness or laziness.

There were once two friends called Duffy and Fluffy. They grew up close to each other and spent their entire first year together swimming, diving and honking at those around them. Did I mention that Fluffy and Duffy were geese?

One cool morning Fluffy and Duffy went swimming amongst the reeds. Usually the two didn't explore far from home. But the two were approaching their first birthdays, and some unknown force was telling them it was time to move. 'I feel like we should be going somewhere soon,' Fluffy said to Duffy.

'I don't know,' Duffy said. 'I think that first we should talk to our parents. I wouldn't want to get in trouble.'

Just then three loud pops were heard followed by the loud honking and flapping of a gaggle of geese in flight. The two young geese were scared and hid in the thick reeds to wait until the coast was clear. When they returned, their families were nowhere in sight. 'What should we do?' Duffy asked Fluffy. The two agreed that they should wait a day or two for their parents' return. After two days and no sign of their families, Fluffy said, 'It's time to keep moving south. I think that is where our families went. I don't know why, but something inside me tells me to go south.'

'No,' Duffy said. 'That would be too risky. What if they aren't there? What if we leave and tomorrow they come looking for us and we aren't here? I'm not leaving this pond.'

'But it's been getting colder every day. We shall surely die if we stay here. I'm flying south. If you want to stay here alone, then that is your decision.'

And for the first time in their lives, the two geese were separated. Fluffy flew south – chased by a bitter cold northern – into the unknown.

The same north cold that nipped at Fluffy's tail feathers enclosed on Duffy and the small lake which he decided to call home. The reeds, which were plump and full as a child, had now shed their seeds and bent naked in the cold arctic winds. The lake began to freeze over, and soon Duffy had only a small patch of water to swim in.

'I should have gone south with Fluffy,' Duffy thought. 'If only I would have gone. I'm too weak to fly through this weather now; it's far too cold. Fluffy was always a smarter goose than me anyways.'

A week a later the lake completely enclosed on Duffy freezing him in place, leaving him trapped in the decisions that he made.

Further south Fluffy had found his family resting worriedly on a large playa lake. The happy reunion was short-lived when all realized that Fluffy flew in alone. As Fluffy told his story, how he and Duffy had been scared in the reeds, how they had waited for two days for their families return, how Duffy was too scared to leave, the elder geese listened attentively.

'Sometimes,' they said, 'it is the ability to start a journey which makes all the difference. Deep inside one knows what should be done. It is the doing which makes all the difference.'

Research conclusively shows that people must learn to handle procrastination better.

Whether your life is hectic or relatively slow at the time, it is always easy to make excuses and procrastinate. The procrastinator is generally quite sure that he has plenty of time to complete the task at hand. Armed with many forms of expression to make his claims seem legitimate, the procrastinator may say, 'we don't have the time right now. I will get around to it later. Let me sleep on it first. There is lots of time to do that this weekend.' Why do we procrastinate?

> *The leading rule for the lawyer, as for the man of every*
> *other calling, is diligence. Leave nothing for to-morrow*
> *which can be done to-day.*
>
> **–Abraham Lincoln**

A doctor turned to his patient and said, 'Bill, I have some bad news and some worse news.'

'Hold on now doctor,' said the concerned patient. 'I can handle bad news and good news but bad news and worse news?'

The doctor asked which one he should share first. Bill wanted the bad news first.

'Well,' the doctor said sadly, 'The results of all the tests are in and you have only 24 hours to live.'

'What? That's the bad news? What could possibly be worse than that?'

The doctor replied apologetically, 'We found out yesterday and didn't know how to tell you.'

There are infinite reasons to procrastinate. If the procrastinator took the time to work on what needed to be done instead of making excuses, the task would be completed quickly. It is easy to put off unpleasant, difficult and time-consuming tasks. Some people are just easily overwhelmed. They may say, 'It's too hard' or 'No one else has to do it.' Others are self-doubting; they don't believe they are capable of succeeding, so they put it off. When they procrastinate to the point of failure, it reinforces their notion that they are failures when they are actually just scared to start. The main reason is quite simple: it just seems easier to procrastinate. In fact, procrastination is nothing more than a time waster. It causes many more headaches than it cures.

> *Anyone can do any amount of work providing it isn't the work he is supposed to be doing at that moment.*
>
> **–Robert Benchley**

Therefore, we do only those tasks that scream the most, as it were. We rush to finish them. The minute we lick the envelope we notice we forgot to insert the letter. We start cooking hamburgers only to remember the BBQ gas tank is empty. There is a cure for procrastination! Look in a mirror and you will see the cure. The only person who will manage you is YOU!

Procrastination is a strange phenomenon. It often seems to be a good solution for making life more enjoyable (by delaying unpleasant responsibilities). However, procrastination almost invariably works to make things ultimately more difficult and stressful. In addition, it is a rare individual who escapes the dark hand of procrastination. Many people struggle for years to free themselves from its chains in order to forge ahead towards academic success, fulfilling relationships, a clean house or a muscular body.

Leaving bills for another day is a common procrastination mistake that gets people into trouble. If you don't have the money to pay the full bill, call the company and explain. Tell them how much you can pay, or work out smaller monthly payments. You know it will show up next month. But this time it will be larger and harder to pay than the one that came before.

To rid yourself of debt you must not focus on debt. The Law of Attraction states that what you put your energy into will manifest itself into your life. By focusing on your debt, more debt will come. It has to because of the universal laws. Instead, think of how you will make money. Don't think of the debt. By putting all of your energy into making more money, money will come your way. When you have more money, you will be able to pay off your debt. It is that simple.

What does procrastination accomplish? Some say nothing. I say it accomplishes a lot. It finds any way possible to sabotage your life and accomplishes its goal of dragging you farther and farther away from your goals.

Procrastination follows the same rules as everything else in the universe. By thinking of putting off your tasks, you will undoubtedly procrastinate because that is where you are putting your mental energy. Don't think about procrastinating. Instead, plan your day. Think of each step and in what order you want these steps accomplished, and your day will unfold just as you planned. If you keep the vision of your day in your head, it will manifest itself into reality.

Most people understand that they will feel better once their duties are done. But the human brain is infinitely complex, and procrastination is not an easy monster to beat. It is not necessarily the result of laziness or lack of self-discipline; it can be rooted in a multiplicity of causes. In addition, determining why you procrastinate is the best way to eradicate it from your list of habits. Once you've learned why you put things off, you can deal with the real issues at hand and finally learn to face work and school, to deal with relationships, to tackle household chores and to face personal issues head on. With a good attitude, faith and perseverance, this battle can be won!

> *In moment of decision, the best thing you can do is the*
> *right thing to do. The worst thing you can do is nothing.*

> **–Theodore Roosevelt**

Here are some methods being used by major corporations to curb the time problems.

Strategies for Success

Procrastination Strategy 1: Start the Task

How wonderful it is that nobody need wait a single moment before starting to improve the world.

–Anne Frank

Begin the task at hand. If you don't start, you will never be able to finish. Get going, even if you have failed at it in the past. If you want to win, you must begin. This seems obvious, but if you have been procrastinating at something, just make a start at it and you will have begun the process of success.

If you are trying to lose weight or exercise more often, immediately go out and obtain what you will need to begin. Buy running shoes and clothes made especially for working out. By doing this you are setting in motion a chain of events that will eventually lead to success. Once you have obtained everything you need, you will be left only with the next part of the equation that ends in your goal.

Think of an avalanche. Snow can sit on a mountain for years and not move an inch. Millions of tonnes of snow are stuck on a slope held down by nothing more than friction. One single snowflake or one tiny vibration is all it takes to release a chain reaction that ends in an avalanche that can wipe out whole forests. It doesn't take a nuclear bomb to move this mass of snow down the mountain, just the miniscule weight of a tiny snowflake.

You will see this happen in your life as well. Like the avalanche, your life needs only a small change in it to start a chain reaction. Start with the process and, before you know it, your life will build and build until it has enough energy to tackle even the most massive of forests that may lie between you and your goals.

Procrastination Strategy 2: Block off Time

I don't wait for moods. You accomplish nothing if you do
that. Your mind must know it has got to
get down to work.

–Pearl S. Buck

Make time to get the task done. Chances are remote that you will ever get a task done without it getting scheduled into your calendar. We procrastinate forever because we don't block off the necessary time to finish the job.

When our days are busy, we can easily put off or forget changes that we have implicated in our day-to-day living. Put a few calendars around the house in places where you will see them often. One in the bedroom, kitchen and bathroom will do. When you see your goals, often they will stay in your mind and will begin to occur, in accordance with the Law of Attraction. Scheduling your goals along with your other responsibilities makes them real. When you see that you need groceries, you are sure to go buy them because you need to eat. Don't sleep until the schedule you have made for yourself is completed each day. Don't view this as an intimidating thing. Don't say, 'It will be impossible to accomplish all this in a day.' By saying this, you make it so. Tell yourself, 'This is what I will do today,' and, due to the Law of Attraction, you will.

Procrastination Strategy 3: See the Job in Bite-Sized Pieces

Even if you're on the right track, you'll get run over if you just sit there.

–Arthur Godfrey

You will never start losing weight if you see the whole project in one lump sum. Don't look too far into the future. The whole task itself may seem overwhelming, but in pieces it won't seem as hard. An alcoholic would have difficulty picturing himself not drinking for the rest of his life. He can handle not drinking for this-24-hour period. 'One day at a time' is a popular slogan among self-help groups.

Sticking with the exercising example, picturing yourself running a marathon may seem like flying to the moon. Begin by running short distances. After running a mile for a week, two miles won't seem impossible. After running two miles for a while, three won't seem so tough. Before you know it, you will be running distances that you never would have imagined from the cushions of your sofa.

Procrastination Strategy 4: Adopt a 'Do-It-Now' Mentality

In delay there lies no plenty.

–William Shakespeare

People who conquer procrastination problems learn that when you think something should be done, DO IT. They never wait until tomorrow to do what they know should be done today. They put things back after each use. They refuse to delay. Even the small things can add up. Do everything you can and need to do today and your life will become less stressful.

We will discuss action in detail in chapter 10, but I will briefly talk about it here as well. If something needs to be done, it will remain in the 'need-to-do' box until it is completed. Mark off tasks on your schedule after they are completed. Those that are not completed will roll over to the next day, making a day that was already filled to the brim spill over. It is always to your benefit to complete everything you can.

Procrastination Strategy 5: Set up Objectives

I love deadlines. I like the whooshing sound they make as they fly by.

–Douglas Adams

We have already discussed the need for objectives in life, but it bears repeating here, as it affects the procrastination dilemma. Set a goal to accomplish something you have put off doing, and actively work on reaching it. Your schedule and lists from Step 4 will help you to actively achieve your objective.

Simplify your life. You do not need all the clutter you are holding on to. Get rid of it now because it is stealing your energy. The clutter in your life takes energy to maintain. Start with the smallest things. Clear away a little, and you'll be amazed at the vast amounts of energy it releases inside of you.

Clutter can be something as small as old clothes and junk you hold on to around the house, to something as large as friends that are holding you down. You are taking a giant step in your life, and putting yourself on the line takes strength. Any extra baggage that you drag along will only help bring you down. If you are trying to feel better about yourself by exercising, get rid of all the old clothes that you believe make you look bad and replace them with the clothes you want to wear. If the people you surround yourself with help you stay in the same ruts that you've always been in, don't waste time around them so often. Maybe you should consider hanging around with people that you would like to be like.

Set your goals and attack them day by day. Soon you will pull back and realize that the life you once led is just that, a previous dream life. You will be amazed that you allowed yourself to live that way and proud at where you are standing the in world at the moment. It will be a great moment.

Procrastination Strategy 6: Review Accomplishments

*He who puts off nothing till tomorrow has done
a great deal.*

–Baltasar Graci

Winners in life dwell on their successes. Losers constantly focus in on their failures. Don't focus on the times you have failed. It is of value to remind yourself of areas you have succeeded in winning the procrastination game.

Nobody has ever accomplished every task they have tried, every time. It is ridiculous to think that you can succeed on the first try with everything you do. There will be many times when you have to try multiple times before you finally accomplish your goal. It takes a strong mentality to forget failures and constantly look towards the great that rests in the future.

The best way to strengthen your mental muscle is to think of all the times you have succeeded. If a task seems insurmountable, think of a time when you accomplished a goal against all odds. This will instil the belief in you that you can do whatever you put your mind to, which is the truth.

Procrastination Strategy 7: Reward or Punish Yourself

*It is not because things are difficult that we do not dare,
it is because we do not dare that they are difficult.*

–Seneca

I am not espousing weird behaviour by suggesting you conquer procrastination problems by physically punishing yourself. What I am suggesting is that you find some way of punishing negative behaviours, such as not doing things you said you would do. Find a negative reinforcement for a negative behaviour and a positive reinforcement for a positive one.

One manager I know buys all his staff lunch, out of his own pocket, if he does not have his reports in on time. If he promises to deliver something and procrastinates, he has to fork out cash, and for him this is negative reinforcement for negative behaviour.

If you fail to deliver on a task, don't go to that restaurant you were dying to go to. Take away little pleasures when you fail, and you will soon realize how much you take them for granted.

If you succeed in a task, reward yourself in moderation. Take family or friends to a nice dinner out, or reward yourself with something that you have been wanting. Don't go out of control; you will begin to associate positive actions with positive results.

Procrastination is the art of keeping up with yesterday
and avoiding today.

–Wayne Dyer

Postpone not a good action.

–Irish Proverb

Don't wait. The time will never be just right.

–Napoleon Hill

Chapter 5

You Are in Control

Turning Yourself on to Self-Discipline

Strategy 1: Master Your Habits

Bad habits are hard to break. That statement is both true and false. True in the sense that before we know it something that we thought we could easily master or control is now much more difficult. It is a false statement because I do not believe any habit is unbreakable. Every habit can be subjected to our control. Controlling bad habits leads the list for ways to save time.

Show me any person with a strong sense of self-control, and I'll show you a winner. Conversely, a loser has little control.

The high achievers in life have a common denominator: they have mastered their habits. Look for a minute at the poor achievers in life; the opposite is true of them. The under-achievers have failed miserably because they lack self-discipline. They always let things slip. They seem to have not given enough attention and concern for the important things in life. What they don't know is that the easy way out does very little, if anything, to help change and make them a better person.

There were once two squirrels named Tiki and Taco. Tiki loved to play in the trees and lie in the sun. Taco also enjoyed playing and napping in the warm sun, but he also spent a few hours a day finding and storing acorns.

'Come collect acorns with me,' Taco said. 'It will soon be winter and you will be upset that you don't have food.'

'There are plenty of acorns out. I will gather them later, but today I'm going to lie in the sun. It is such a pretty day. I wouldn't want to waste it,' Tiki said.

So day after day Tiki played in the trees and napped in the sun. Taco continued spending a few hours a day collecting, storing and planning for the winter months ahead. In the evening Taco expressed his concerns to Tiki. 'Tiki, what will you do when winter comes? You haven't been taking this seriously. Do you think life is one big game? All you do is play and sleep.' Tiki only laughed and told Taco not to worry.

One day the winter winds came and stripped all the remaining acorns from the trees. The squirrels scrambled to grab the last of the acorns while Tiki slept on a bed of dried grass. When he awoke, he was shocked to see that all the acorns were gone and all the squirrels were huddled up in the trees. He ran quickly to Taco's tree and pleaded with him, 'Taco, you must give me some acorns or else I'll starve this winter.'

'I will give you one acorn a day,' he said. 'I shouldn't give you one single acorn, but since you are my friend I will help you.'

'I can barely live on one acorn a day,' Tiki said.

'You will be hungry all winter, and maybe you will learn your lesson,' Taco said. 'Next summer, maybe instead of sleeping and playing all day, you will get your habits under control. Maybe now you will understand that life isn't just one big game.'

Some people seem to have chosen the path of least resistance. They have tried to take the easy way out because it meant less work on the hard things in life, namely change and control of oneself. Who are the most productive and successful people you know? Would they be characterized as people who have mastered habits? Are they highly disciplined people? How many people do you really know whom you would label 'highly disciplined?' Can you name ten? Five? Two? I bet each one lives a successful life.

Delayed Gratification

Delayed gratification is the delaying of the reward or pleasure phase and counting on, even scheduling, the investment or problem phase first to more fully enjoy the benefits later. It's getting the unpleasant task done first to enjoy the gratification more deeply later.

Would Michael Jordan have won as many championships if he missed workouts or didn't invest his life in basketball? When the games came, he wouldn't have been prepared to hit those last minute, game-winning shots that he became so famous for. Jordan wouldn't be the champion he is today without delaying certain pleasures.

How far would Wayne Gretzky have got if he had tried to put the blessing or victory phase before the workout or investment phase? When the games came, he wouldn't have got very far without the early morning runs and late night practices. There was no way he could have handled the game without delaying certain pleasures to more fully enjoy the victory phase later.

Delayed gratification means working on problems NOW. It may be tough; sure, it will be stretching; but you agree that for you to really enjoy the pleasure or payoff phase, you will work hard first. You sow now so you can reap later.

Strategy 2: Make a List of All the Habits You Would Like to Change in the Next Two Years

If you are like most salespeople I speak with, you probably wish you were more disciplined. Many times a day you might think critically of yourself for postponing (sometimes indefinitely!) those things that you know you want to change. There are certain things you know you should stop doing, yet you never seem to tackle them. There are certain other habits you know you should start doing but have failed to begin.

The psychological cost for salespeople is far too great to be living in that vast wasteland called 'Lack of Discipline.' You know exactly what you need to do. For some reason – perhaps lack of motivation, lack of initiative or not having a plan – you have permitted yourself and your life to become cluttered with undesirable habits. The time to change all that is now!

Strategy 3: Follow the Six-Step
Process for Developing Discipline in Your Life

Step 1: Identify one habit or area you would like to become more disciplined in. The first step is to identify one specific behaviour you would like to change. It should be written as a behaviour. It should describe something you now do that you would like to stop doing or something you now don't do consistently and would like to do regularly. You can use this step to describe the outcome you would like to accomplish. You must, however, confine each worksheet to one specific issue or behaviour. Attempting to do too much may be discouraging. Each worksheet will take you through this six-step process. It applies only to one issue per worksheet.

Step 2: Find role models. Ask yourself, who is doing it right? By identifying one or more people who have discipline in this area, you will see that if others can do it, so can you. The people you list in this section need not be personal acquaintances. You may not know them personally at all. They may be alive or dead. The point here is to cause you to think about specific people who you believe have or had control in this area, people you will emulate. Ask or figure out how they live or lived as they did or do. You will be able to set some guidelines from their lives to help you live your own.

Too many of us seek advice from those who know nothing about what we want to accomplish. Why do we put our trust and faith in those who aren't qualified to assist us? Unless a friend or family member is accomplished and a positive role model in your area of interest, don't have that person help you. You may have obtained guidance from that person over the years, but where has this advice taken you? If you want advice on property investment, for example, why would you ask someone who wasn't rich and successful from property investing? Never trust the advice of a person in difficulties.

There is an old story about a fox and a goat. One day the fox was walking along the edge of a cliff looking for water, as there had been a long drought, when he slipped and fell into a well. The fox tried and tried to scale the walls of the well but could not get out.

A while later the goat came by and, being sure footed, was able to not slip into the well. The goat looked down and saw the fox lying on the ground. The goat asked, 'Fox, what are you doing way down there in that well?'

To which the fox replied, 'It will rain soon, and when it does, I will be in this well to drink all the water that collects here. You are welcome to come down here and join me, but you cannot tell anyone else.'

The goat thought for a moment and, because he knew the fox was so smart, decided to join him in the well. The goat jumped down next to the fox, and the two sat side by side in the bottom of the well. 'Thanks for inviting me down,' the goat said. 'The drought has been long, and I could sure use some water.'

Just then the fox jumped on the back of the goat and, running up the goat's long spiralling horns, jumped out of the well to freedom. The goat sat stunned, still trapped at the bottom of the well. 'What are you doing?' the goat pleaded. 'I thought you said we would drink water at the bottom of this well together.'

'Goodbye my friend,' the fox said. 'I hope you have learned your lesson.'

Step 3: *List the benefits of becoming self-disciplined in this area.* Now ask yourself, what's in it for me? You want to consider why you want to develop in this area. By listing the rewards, you will be willing to work harder. You need to feel, smell, taste, see and touch exactly what it will be like once you are strong in this area.

Write about how your life will be once you have achieved your goals. What will a typical day be like? How will you act? Seeing the life you want on paper will turn your goals into more than a dream. You will have a concrete representation that you can read when you hit an obstacle.

This step gets you to focus on the benefits of becoming disciplined in this area. You could consider listing the pain of NOT becoming disciplined here.

Step 4: *Consider the danger zones.* You now need to consider where you might fall. You need to give some thought to the danger zones. You know that if you are going to become more disciplined, you will be tempted to fall off the wagon, to be led astray, to procrastinate. If you have been attempting to become more self-disciplined for some time, you know that for you there is a pattern of failure to comply. What happens to you? You start off strongly and then before you know it, you are doing the very things you said you wouldn't or you have stopped doing the things you said you would and know you should.

What you need to find out is where, what, when and why. Where were you when you failed last? What were you doing? What made you fail? When was this last time? Why did you fail? By answering these questions, you can have a better understanding about what makes you slip, what makes you walk backwards. Think about how you could've handled the situation differently, and next time you are there act accordingly.

By acknowledging that you have fallen in the past, you can better plan for your future. It takes great strength to admit your weaknesses. Tell the people in your support system about the things that have brought you down before. The more they know, the stronger they will be.

Step 5: Use advanced decision making. You cannot win in life if you are controlled by whimsical or situational decision making. If you are to succeed in life, you will need to consider in advance how you will live your life.

In this step you will need to give some thought to what specific actions you will need to take to accomplish the goal listed in Step 1. For example, if you wanted to become more disciplined in the area of exercise, one decision made in advance could be to decide to exercise every morning upon waking for 45 minutes while watching a video workout DVD. Or you may decide to run every other evening after work and go to the gym the other nights.

You decide in advance that you will do this. You don't wait until the morning to see if you feel like doing it. You have already decided how you will live your life.

Tiger Woods doesn't wake up and say he doesn't feel like practicing. He gets up and does it. He hits balls before and after every round, regardless of its outcome. Can you imagine hitting 100 golf balls after winning a major tournament? Tiger Woods does. And that is why he is the greatest golfer alive, maybe the greatest golfer of all time.

Tiger Woods does this because he knows that if he wants to be the best, he has to put in the extra effort and not make excuses. He even won the U. S. Open playing on a broken leg. Some say that he has the strongest mental makeup of any athlete alive.

Step 6: Enrol a support team. This step is by far one of the most crucial. If you don't do this step, you are cheating yourself out of the real power behind this system. It is vital for you to finally become the strong and self-disciplined person you know you can and should be. Resist the temptation to avoid this step because it may be different from what you are used to or even uncomfortable. It will literally change your life.

This step asks you to enlist the assistance of someone you respect to help you become disciplined in this area. Here's what you do. First, you need to think of someone who you respect and someone who will be strong enough to hold you to certain decisions about becoming disciplined. You call this person and tell him or her that you have identified certain areas you are looking to becoming more disciplined in. You are going to send this person a copy of the worksheet and would like him or her to hold you accountable to the actions and decisions on the sheet.

This will force you to do what you said you would and know you should. Find someone to call you at least once a week. Allow yourself to become accountable to this person. This has literally transformed my life and that of my students worldwide.

Strategy 4: Avoid the Three Lies

Watch for the three lies of the Habit Demons. Every time a person breaks a commitment and falls back into a bad habit that person has bought into one of the three lies of the Habit Demons.

Think back to when you started a bad habit. Think about what happens to every alcoholic who falls off the wagon or a person who gains back the weight he has lost or someone who wastes piles of time dealing with issues he once had under control. Think about the people you know who have relapsed into their bad habits; it only takes one lie for them to get back into their old ways. Losing a bad habit is tough, but falling back into the same old groove is too easy. These three lies rear their ugly heads; we buy into them and then fall.

Lie 1: *Once will be enough*. 'I'll have just one beer, one smoke, one dessert.' Anytime you hear something inside that sounds like that, it's Lie 1. Is one beer enough for an alcoholic? No, one is too many and a thousand is not enough. Whenever you hear 'once' or 'just this time,' let a red flag remind you about the Habit Demons' lies, or you will soon be back into your old ways.

Lie 2: *Mess it up good*. Once you give in to Lie 1 and do something you know you shouldn't, Lie 2 kicks in. 'Now that I've blown it, I'll mess it up good.' It looks like this for someone trying to control the bad habit of eating late at night. 'I'll have just one piece of pie. One little piece can't hurt me. I deserve just one small piece.' So you start cutting yourself a piece. Soon afterwards you hear Lie 2. 'Well, now that I've done it, I might as well have another piece now. Wouldn't another piece taste great? I've blown it, so why not mess it up good? Go ahead, have another piece, and why not top it off with some vanilla ice cream?' You give in and feel terrible. Then comes Lie 3, the final stage of loss of control.

Lie 3: *Give up*. By giving in and doing what you did not want to do, you feel terrible. You have messed it up good, so now the natural progression is to stop trying, to simply give up. This lie tries to get you to say, 'I'm worthless. I'm hopeless, and I will never be able to control my habits. I'll quit trying.'

Reject all three lies; they are false. Once is rarely enough. If you are tempted to do something wrong once, check out if it's not the first of the three lies. If you do mess something up, don't mess it up even more. You don't have to go any further. You can resume control. Exercise that control now. Never believe Lie 3; never quit trying. You are of immense value; you are never hopeless. The winners in life recognize and refute the lies of the Habit Demons.

No man is a loser until he quits trying.

Chapter 6

Self-Confidence

How to Unleash Your Power Centre

The Power Key to Your Fabulous Future

Two women are in a personnel office about to be interviewed for the same job. They are both responding to an ad they saw in the local newspaper. They both have children and both are returning to work after being away from the job market for 15 years. Both women want this job.

Lucy sits nervously, fidgeting while she waits for the personnel manager to call her in. Once in the office, she sits rigidly, looking very pale, her hands sweating and trembling somewhat. She is breathing shallowly; her heart is racing; she finds it difficult to look the interviewer in the eye.

'Lucy, you have read the ad, you've applied for this job and you have certain skills. What makes you think you are qualified? In a nutshell, why should I hire you?'

Before she even opens her mouth, Lucy has a terrible sinking feeling in the pit of her stomach. She asks herself what she is doing here. Already she feels embarrassed for even having applied for the job. She's ashamed. She feels dejected and flustered. 'I guess I was sick of just staying home. I was bored with housework. You see, the kids are in school all day and I need something to do. I've cooked some and I've cleaned some.' As Lucy mouths those empty words, she is filled with self-doubt and self-hatred. The thought of even trying to enter the competitive job market at her age repulses her. She feels she has blown the interview and leaves the office totally humiliated, vowing never to put herself through that type of embarrassment again.

The second woman, Jane, has exactly the same qualifications. She too has been out of the job market for almost 15 years. Her children have grown and her experience is that of a mother and homemaker.

She walks into the personnel manager's office with a bounce in her step. She smiles at him, looks him straight in the eye and takes a seat, sitting in a confident posture.

The manager asks her the same question he asked Lucy: 'Jane, you have read the ad, you've applied for this job and you have certain skills. What makes you think you are qualified? In a nutshell, why should I hire you?'

Sitting up straight in her chair she responds by saying, 'Mr Jones I would like you to know a little about me. I've been a housewife for the past 15 years, and I think it has made me uniquely qualified to fill this position. I have personally tutored four children all the way through grammar and grade school. I have done their homework with them and helped them. I know all about maths and English. I have been a counsellor to my kids in each area of life from college choice to dating. I am the right person for the job.

'Over the past 15 years, I have been a domestic engineer, a purchasing agent and a cook, and I have been instrumental in keeping my home intact. This is no easy thing in our day. For the past 15 years, I have been a meal planner, nurse, police officer, judge, jury, wardrobe consultant, budget expert, financial planner, teacher, tutor, cheerleader, spiritual adviser, maid, linguistics expert, gardener, administrator, schedule planner, chauffeur, environmentalist and family traditionalist.

'For my husband I have been a friend, a lover, an adviser, an encourager, a partner, a comforter and a constant companion. For my community I have been a caring neighbour, a diligent volunteer, a giving friend and a church member.

'Mr Jones, with that vast amount of experience, I have gained an incredible amount of knowledge and skill. Given a little time and training, I am absolutely convinced I can do this job and do it well.'

Which one do you think will probably get the job? The facts were almost the same for both women. Why would the outcome be so dramatically different? What did Jane have that Lucy lacked? The answer is self-confidence. One was sure of herself; the other doubted herself. If we want to have more confidence to succeed, we need to remove questions of self-doubt that attempt to sabotage our goal achievements. Attitude, after all, is everything.

Self-Confidence Booster 1: Identify ten people you consider as self-confident. List what makes them so. Self-confidence isn't something only a few of us should have. I believe that everyone should be self-confident no matter where you are from or what you do for a living. The potential for self-confidence is inside everyone. Think of ten people who you consider self-confident. Make a list of what makes them that way. Where are they the most confident? Why are they that way? How did they achieve this?

Name of confident person	How does that person show it?
1.	
2.	
3.	
4.	
5.	
6.	
7.	
8.	
9.	
10.	

If you are not confident in yourself, how can you be confident in anything that you do? You have to believe 100 per cent in what you are doing to succeed. You can never believe in what you are doing if you don't believe in yourself, as every action you make reflects who and what you are.

Self-Confidence Booster 2: Understand the difference between self-esteem and self-confidence. Self-esteem and self-confidence are similar but concerned with two very different things. Self-esteem attempts to answer the question: do I matter? Self-esteem deals with you as a person. Self-esteem is more a question of self-worth. Self-confidence deals with do I have skills? The latter is concerned with ability; the former, with worth.

The following are necessary ingredients to develop healthy self-confidence.

Security

Security is a very important thing when building self-confidence. We all should know that rain or shine, sink or swim, fail or succeed our friends and family will always be there to support us. And with the support of those around us, we will remain strong and unable to fail.

Let me share an Aesop fable with you. A father had sons who were perpetually quarrelling among themselves. When he failed to heal their disputes by his exhortations, he determined to give them a practical illustration of the evils of disunion; and for this purpose he one day told them to bring him a bundle of sticks. When they had done so, he placed the bundle into the hands of each of them in succession and ordered them to break it in pieces. They tried with all their strength and were not able to do it. He next opened the bundle, took the sticks separately one by one and again put them into his sons' hands, upon which they broke them easily. He then addressed them in these words: 'My sons, if you are of one mind and unite to assist each other, you will be as this bundle, uninjured by all the attempts of your enemies. But if you are divided among yourselves, you will be broken as easily as these sticks.'

Your relationship with your loved ones didn't begin based on performance, so why would it end that way?

If you are to develop self-confidence, you need to understand that you have a security net. If you fall, relationships will still be there to bring you back up.

Opportunity

Self-confidence is concerned with ability. A necessary ingredient, therefore, in this area is opportunity to prove and test your abilities. When you are in a moment in your life when you are confident, you shine most as a person. If you are good at a sport, you will be excited to get together with others and play. If you doubt your abilities in the game, you may keep quiet and stand at the back of the crowd, hoping that the topic will shift to something you are more confident with.

There will be many situations in your life where you can either sit on the sidelines or step up and show your skills. If you know that you can do something, do it. Your confidence in yourself will grow, as will others' confidence in you. When you have confidence, others will have confidence in you.

Erin was getting older and felt that her family wasn't including her in activities because of her age. When games were played or things needed to be done, no one ever asked her to get involved, so Erin just sat and watched as others in her family began to do all the tasks she could do so well. They played badminton without her, drove her around when the family went to dinner and even began making her famous guacamole.

One day Erin was watching her grandchildren play badminton in her backyard. Suddenly she got out of her chair and walked over to the younger of the two boys and took his racket. The elder boy laughed, 'Grandma, what are you doing?' he asked.

'Just serve the shuttlecock,' she said with a grin.

The boy served the shuttle, and Erin proceeded to beat the pants off of her eldest grandchild. At the end of the match, her grandchildren came up to her in amazement. 'I didn't know you could play badminton,' they all said.

'There are many things that Grandma can do that you don't know about,' she said.

'We could have been playing together for years,' they said. And from then on, the challenge among the boys wasn't who could beat Grandma; it was who could score the most points against Grandma.

Erin had missed out on years of fun with her grandchildren because she never took the opportunity to join them in a sport that she knew she was good at. The attitudes of others influenced her self-confidence, and she let this rule her life and affect her way of thinking.

This is how your confidence shows. An interviewer can see the people who are excited and the people hiding in the crowd. Who do you think she will pick?

What area of your life would you consider yourself fairly self-confident in? Would you say you have had a recent positive experience in that area? Sure, we are confident in the areas we do well in. If we win certain battles, we are confident in facing others. It's like the marine officer when he saw that he and his men were surrounded by the enemy and said, 'Men, we are surrounded on all sides; don't let one of them get away.' We have certain abilities and we can test them out in the forum of life.

Acknowledgement

To grow into self-confident individuals, we need the acknowledgment that says you are super; that was fantastic; you matter; you did a great job.

We all need to be reminded that we are special. We need it from others and from ourselves. Don't let a good deed go unrewarded. If you or someone close to you accomplishes something towards a goal, acknowledge this with praise. We appreciate positive feedback and recognition for a job well done no matter what our age. If you begin praising your friends and family for their accomplishments, they will do the same in return, and you will rise together.

Self-acknowledgement is just as important as acknowledgement from others.

Self-Confidence Booster 3: Specify your skills. What are you competent at? What are some things you do fairly well? There is no such answer as, nothing to that question. I refuse to accept that and so should you. It is a blatant lie to answer that question by saying who me? I can't do anything well. That's baloney. Look a little deeper.

We all have certain strengths and abilities whether in knowledge, character, experience or personality traits. Specify what you are good at. Repeat those things to yourself and start doing more of those things that are positive for you.

Do you have any of the following qualities?

___ Care about others	___ Detail orientated
___ Good with numbers	___ Strong willed
___ Woodworking skills	___ Good cook
___ Sing well	___ Creative
___ Listen to others	___ Good swimmer
___ Organizer	___ Write poetry
___ Know languages	___Good speaker
___ Can drive a truck	___ Know CPR
___ Have a hobby	___ Good at a game
___ Play a musical instrument	___ Handyman
___ Travel experience	___ Love people
___ Love for animals	___ Honest
___ Know someone famous	___ Hard worker
___ Have an interesting collection	___ Smart
___ Work diligently	___ Have integrity

Self-Confidence Booster 4: Stretch your competencies. Self-confidence is nothing more than knowledge. Let me say that in a different way. To be self-confident, all you need is information. Look at it this way. You do something well 5000 times. You know you can do it. If you've done it right that many times, you know you can do it; therefore, you are confident. If you have never done it before, then you don't KNOW.

Without that knowledge, you doubt. If you want to be confident, give yourself the chance to find out what your abilities are. By trying new things and taking the risk to stretch your present level of ability, you discover that trying is the key. You come to know that taking a chance is not the end of the world. You realize that security and peace are not the grounds on which self-confidence is developed. Without at least trying, you are living well below your ability level.

Self-doubt is a progressive illness. When you refuse to risk and try confidence-building projects, you begin the downwards spiral of rejecting growth opportunities and settling instead for the safety net of life.

That pattern is the 'safety-net syndrome.' You refuse to leave the nest; you don't try anything that in anyway threatens the security and safety factors.

I'm sure you have heard the phrase sink or swim sometime in your life. This phrase brings to mind a child learning to swim. You put the child in the water, and he either swims or sinks. Of course, this is not true. No one would ever let the child sink, but this is where the phrase originated from.

The key is to just get in the pool and try your hardest. Get in and do something you've never tried before with the sink-or-swim mentality. Just like the child in the pool, you won't sink. Your support system is always there to help you. The more things you accomplish in life, the more confident you will be in yourself and your abilities.

When was the last time you tried something you've never done before? When were you last exposed to some growth opportunity? By taking some risk and succeeding, you create that pattern of stretching your ability and increasing your knowledge of your skill level. What kind of risk taker are you?

Self-Confidence Booster 5: Get help if needed. Some people feel a need to cover up a lack of self-confidence by trying to make a big impression. A newly promoted army colonel moved into his new and impressive office. As he sat behind his new big desk, a private knocked at his door.

'Just a minute,' the colonel said, 'I'm on the phone.' He picked up the receiver and said loudly, 'Yes sir, general. I'll call the prime minister this afternoon. No sir, I won't forget.' Then he hung up the phone and told the private to come in. 'What can I help you with?'

'Well, sir,' the private replied, 'I've come to hook up that phone.'

There is help available to assist in giving you some positive success experience. People who fear public speaking have become confident speakers by joining a Toastmasters club. Toastmasters provides the platform and opportunity to stretch your competencies. If you want to get more self-confidence, you should join Toastmasters International. The cost is minimal compared to the immense value of the organization. To find a club in your area, look in the telephone book or go the organization's website, www.toastmasters.org. Toastmasters is only one organization dedicated to helping develop your self-confidence. There are thousands. Find one that's right for you. Don't be so proud that you can't ask for help. Refuse to be like the man who said, 'I by my stupidity got into this mess; therefore, I by my stupidity will get out of it.'

Be careful of the 'if-only syndrome.' This excuse-giving behaviour attempts to put off self-development by coming up with reasons to delay.

If only I had a boyfriend.

If only I had more money.

If only I were more attractive.

If only I had less stress/more friends/fewer hassles/more creativity/less inflation/more breaks in life.

Self-Confidence Booster 6: Pick five self-confidence tips from the following list and implement them today.

- Join a status-building association, club or organization.

- Meet some important people.

- Buy an expensive suit.

- Do something you are good at 25 times in the next month.

- Write out and repeat self-confidence-building affirmations.

- Spend time with confident people.

- Refuse to host or attend any 'pity parties.'

- Hold your body as a confident person would.

- Remove anything in your life which contributes to self-doubt.

- Take a risk.

- Get on a talk show.

- Start verbalizing that you are a confident person.

- Concentrate on what's right with you.

- Make a list of all your victories, successes and achievements.

- Free yourself from addictions.

- Act confidently.

- Increase your vocabulary.

- Develop an expertise in something.

- Get good at a hobby.

- Take up something unique.

- Read up on a subject that interests your boss.

- Set a small goal and achieve it.

- Help someone less fortunate than yourself.

- Take a risk.

- Create a 'hit list' of influential people you want to meet.

- Buy a book on communication.

- Listen to powerful audio CDs.

- Speak up.

- Give a speech.

- Take an adventurous trip.

- Take a self-defence course.

- Attend a self-esteem seminar.

Be a strong person. Develop a sense of destiny. Know who you are and what you are about. Be proud of who you are and what you will accomplish in this life. When others sense you have strong self-confidence and healthy self-esteem, they will be willing to believe in you, trust and follow you. We are all attracted to dynamic leaders.

Self-Confidence Booster 7: Learn to stand alone. According to industry-wide statistics, at the age of 65, insurance companies calculate that a whopping 94 per cent of North Americans are either dead or dead broke and similar percentages apply for the UK. One out of a hundred is still working. Four are financially stable or just getting by. Out of one hundred people, only one person will be financially independent entering the Golden Years.

> *They plan for the Golden Years, but for far too many of them, it's really the Yearning Years, they are absolutely dependent upon others, even for life's essentials.*

> **–Armando David Vacca**

This is the reality of the masses. For people who want to win at life, breaking away from the masses is an absolute must.

Most people are like a flock of ducks flying across the sky. Very seldom does the duck stop to wonder if the flock is going in the right direction. The duck just falls into line and follows the flock. Doesn't it make sense that a duck that follows the flock will end up exactly where the flock is headed? Of course! In addition, when was the last time that you saw one duck change direction and take off the opposite way? Not too often.

We must understand that the reality of the masses quite simply states that the masses will end up broke and dependent on others for survival. If we follow the flock, that's where we will end up as well. To break this pattern, we must be like the lone duck that turns in the opposite direction and heads away from the flock. Sounds difficult, doesn't it? It is! However, the rewards will pay off for the rest of your life.

Soon you will be flying much higher in the sky, enjoying the life you create, not the one the masses dictate.

Opinions

Why do broke people ask other broke people for opinions or advice on how not to be broke? Heck, if they had any inclination about money, do you think they'd be broke?

Would you go to a gym and get a personal trainer who was overweight and took the elevator to the second floor? You would want a trainer who was in shape and practiced what they preached.

Many people give advice on matters that they struggle with or can't figure out themselves. Would you want to get advice from these people? Don't take advice from the masses or you will end up where the masses are. Take advice from a person who is where you want to be.

Many people live their lives always worried about what their family and friends think of them. Chances are, they don't think at all. That's the problem. They live their lives according to the way they think that their friends and family think that they should live. As soon as someone says

I'm tired of being average, I want to soar with the eagles, the masses, the flock of ducks that they are with, will try to drag them down with their meaningless quacking.

Understand this: what anyone thinks of you is none of your business. At the end of the day, you must answer to yourself. At retirement either you will have the life that you want for your family or you will not. Others will have no solution for you at that point.

As you journey higher into the sky to join the eagles, you will find that there are two basic fears motivating your friends and family to try to stop you. Your family, in most cases, is motivated with good intent. They are living by the mindset of the masses. They are not aware of their own inner strength, let alone yours. Their fear of your failure is greater than their excitement about your success.

You must step out of the mould, despite their advice. Often times your friends, on the other hand, have much more selfish motivations for trying to keep you in the flock. They live by the mindset of the masses as well. They believe that to get ahead in life, one is either lucky or a con artist.

In fact, you may find that the key to success is luck; just ask any failure.

The masses also spend their lives blaming others for their failure. It's the government's fault, it's the recession, it's his fault or it's her fault. Many failures believe that the reason they are where they are is because of their lack of education or opportunity. In truth, none of the above could be further from reality. We are responsible for our own lives. We choose our own pathway to walk by the decisions we make every day.

Tell your friends that you are going to soar with the eagles and make great things happen in your life. You may find that they are not as excited as you are about your new plans. You see, when you become successful, you will shatter the myth that they live their lives by. You instantly force them to accept responsibility for where they are in their lives and for where they are going.

Be strong! Overcome the need you might have to gain the opinions and approval of others. You have decided to move beyond just getting by. You want to better yourself.

Chapter 7

Great Success Demands Great Courage

Risk It

In 1925 a man in Indianapolis, Indiana, in the United States of America, named Herman Krannert was an executive of the Sefton Container Company. On one occasion he was summoned to Chicago to have lunch with the president of the company. He was very excited because he had never been invited to do that before. He went to Chicago to the Athletic Club. While he and the president were having lunch, the president said, 'Herman, I'm going to make an announcement in the company this afternoon that greatly impacts your life. We're going to promote you to senior executive vice president, and you're to be the newest member of the board of directors.'

Krannert was blown away. He said, 'Mr President, I had no idea I was even being considered for this. I want you to know I'll be the most loyal employee this company has ever had. I'm going to dedicate my life to making this the finest corporation in America.'

The president was gratified by this and said, 'You know, Herman, I'm glad you mention that because there's one thing I'd like you remember. As a member of the board of directors, you will vote exactly the way I tell you to.'

That took the wind out of Krannert's sails, and he said he wasn't sure he could do that.

'Come on, Herman, that's the way it is in the business world. I'm putting you on the board of directors. You'll do what I tell you, right?'

The more he thought about that, the angrier Krannert became. At the end of lunch he stood up and said, 'Mr President, I need you to understand I cannot accept this promotion. I will not be a puppet for anybody on a board of directors.' Then he added, 'Not only that, but I won't work for a company where such demands are made. I quit.'

He came back to Indianapolis that night, approached his wife and said, 'You'll be excited to know that today I was promoted to senior executive vice president, made a member of the board of directors and I quit.'

She said, 'You quit? Have you lost your mind?'

However, when he told her what had happened, she was very supportive and said, 'Well, I guess we'll have to find something else.'

Four nights later a knock came at his door. Six senior executives from his company burst through the door, all excited. 'Herman, we heard what happened the other day. We think that's the greatest thing we've ever heard. In fact, we quit too.'

'What do you mean, you quit too?' he said.

'Yeah, we quit too, and here's the good news. We're going to go to work for you!'

'How are you going to work for me? I don't even have a job.'

They said, 'Oh, we figure you'll find something, and when you do, we're going to work for you.'

That night those seven people sat down at Herman Krannert's dining room table and created the Inland Container Corporation. That enterprise exists today because a guy in 1925 knew what he believed in and decided to take a risk.

You got it. Through examples like this one of Herman Krannert and others I am going to share, I want to sell you the idea of risk taking. I want to examine why it's important to be open to risk, to understand why it is so difficult for some people to leave the security of a comfort zone and provide practical suggestions on how you can continue to win big in life by taking risks.

If you are unwilling to risk, you are voting for mediocrity in your life. Let me tell you about another amazing risk taker from London, UK, Mark Smith.

Mark was a very successful banker in London, UK. It is so rare to find someone so dedicated to learning. He grows from all the information obtained from the materials that I have been using to coach people and always attends my seminars and meetings. This man is on fire.

Recently, Mark after attending one of my mastermind meetings decided that he wanted to change his life radically, so he asked me to coach him for six months. Bear in mind that personal coaching is very time consuming and quite expensive. Still, Mark, took a chance, trusted his intuition and went for it.

For six months Mark did everything I asked him to do and intensively studied my material (and all other material that I asked him to study). He claims that this information changed something inside him. He took a big risk and got a big payoff. Taking on personal coaching is not the risk I want to focus on.

After the six months of coaching, Mark decided that he wanted to quit his job and do something productive in his life. He and I met a few extra times to discuss this matter further, as he was extremely anxious about his future.

Like most bankers, Mark got into banking for three reasons: to earn large amounts of money, to benefit from the lavish lifestyle and to meet successful people and benefit from their experience.

Like many people who work for big corporations, Mark had no control of his life and couldn't do his job as he wanted to but had to follow company policies. Mark wanted to build something for himself where he would choose how, when and where he wanted to work. He wanted to regain control of his life.

I suggested that he start up his own business where he would be his own boss, so Mark decided to take an extreme risk. He quit his job, sold his house and his car and even went a step further. He moved halfway across the world to Hong Kong, as he decided that's where he wanted to live, and started up his own business there. This is a frightening risk to anyone, yet he pushed through his terror barrier and made the move. Little did I know that my coaching would have benefited him in such a way! One year now from the move, Mark has never been happier. He is in a great relationship, has made really good friends, and his business is thriving.

Let me bring your attention to some other risk takers.

When slavery was an accepted way to treat people, William Wilberforce stood up in the British Parliament, spoke out against it and began the process of abolishing it. Wilberforce was willing to risk. Think about what it took.

When Rosa Parks refused to go the back of the bus, as was the custom for black people, she risked and won. She ignited the Civil Rights movement in the United States.

When Colonel Sanders refused retirement and founded Kentucky Fried Chicken at the age of 65, he showed he was a risk taker.

When the Singaporean government caned teenager Michael Fay for vandalism in the face of worldwide pressure, they took a risk.

Never Surrender

Never throw in the towel, even against impossible odds or bad luck. There is a host of words in our language that you should concentrate on eliminating from your daily thought. Words such as **can't, impossible, hopeless, futile** carry a negative connotation that works ardently against your success unless you eradicate them from your conscious thoughts. Even the word **luck** denotes the existence of something that we have considerable difficulty defining. The reason for that is because it really does not exist. In the same respect, if you spend your days thinking positively, positive things will occur. There is no such thing as good luck or bad luck; these are only phrases with manmade connotations connected to them. Everything in our lives happens for a reason. Although we don't always realize it, there are thoughts in our minds that actually bring about what happens to us, and luck has nothing to do with it.

More often than not, our desire to give up emanates from a lack of self-confidence or self-esteem. Self-confidence grows with successful accomplishments, even if only small ones, building one on top of another.

The island of Tyre was said to be unconquerable. In 332 BC, Alexander the Great set out to show the power and strength of his army and what he was capable of. Unable to storm the island by land or sea, Alexander blockaded the island for seven months, but Tyre held on. Alexander then used the rubble from an abandoned city to build a bridge and risked going across the water to the island. Every day Alexander added to his path, approaching closer and closer to the island until he was able to walk his army across and surround the city. The unconquerable Tyre fell to Alexander due to his decision, risk taking, persistence and belief that no one in the world could stop him.

You must build your own bridges in life. If Alexander had seen the water and said, I can't, then he would just be Alexander and not Alexander the Great. There will always be obstacles to overcome, but you must always find a way around them and keep moving forwards. When you come upon hard times or seemingly insurmountable obstacles, focus on your one motivating desire to keep moving forwards. Alexander's was to be the ruler of the world and, in essence, yours should be too. Remind yourself of your goals, what you want to achieve and how you are going to get there. By taking the risks, you will create your own path to success.

Chapter 8

Decision

You can make a single mental move which, in a millisecond, will solve enormous problems for you. It has the potential to improve almost any personal or business situation you will ever encounter. It could literally propel you down the path to incredible success. We have a name for this magic mental activity. It is called DECISION.

Once you make a decision, the universe conspires
to make it happen.

–Ralph Waldo Emerson

The world's most successful people share a common quality: they make decisions. Yes, decision makers go to the top while those who do not make decisions seem to go nowhere. THINK ABOUT IT.

Decisions, or lack of them, are responsible for the making or breaking of careers. Individuals who have become proficient at making decisions, without being influenced by the opinions of others, are the same people whose annual incomes falls into the six- and seven-figure category. The person who has never developed the strength to make these mental moves is relegated to the lower income ranks his entire commercial career. And more often than not, his life becomes little more than a dull, boring existence. A Chinese proverb states, 'A wise man makes his own decisions; an ignorant man follows the public ones.'

Not only your income is affected by decisions but your whole life is dominated by this power. The health of your mind and body, the well-being of your family, your social life, the type of relationships you develop are all dependent upon your ability to make sound decisions.

At this point you could be asking yourself, how is a person expected to develop this mental ability? Well, I have the answer for you. You must do it on your own, and you have already begun by thinking about and digesting this information that I am sharing with you. This chapter is causing you to become more aware of the importance of decisions.

You can virtually eliminate conflict and confusion in your life by becoming proficient at making decisions. Decision making brings order to your mind, and, of course, this order is then reflected in your objective world, your results. James Allen, the great Victorian author, might have been thinking of decision when he wrote, 'We think in secret and it comes to pass. Environment is but our looking glass.' No one can see you making decisions, but they almost always see the results of your decisions. The person who fails to develop the ability to make decisions is doomed because indecision sets up internal conflicts, which can, without warning, escalate into all out mental and emotional wars. Psychiatrists have a name to describe these internal wars; it is ambivalence. My Oxford Dictionary tells me that **ambivalence** is 'the co-existence in one person of opposite feelings towards the same objective.'

Everyone on occasion has had feelings of ambivalence. If it happens too frequently, decide right now to stop it. The cause of ambivalence is indecision, but we must keep in mind that the truth is not always in the appearance of things. Indecision may be a cause of ambivalence; however, it is a secondary cause, not a primary cause. I have been studying the behaviour of people who have become proficient at making decisions for more than 20 years. They all have one thing in common. They have a very strong self-image and a high degree of self-esteem. They may be as different as night is to day in numerous other respects, but they certainly possess confidence. Low self-esteem, or a lack of confidence, is the real culprit here. Decision makers are not afraid of making an error. If they make an error in their decision or fail at something, they have the ability to shrug it off. They learn from experience, but they never submit to failure.

All decision makers either were fortunate enough to have been raised in an environment where decision making was part of their upbringing or developed the ability themselves later. They are aware of something that everyone who hopes to live a full life must understand: decision making is something you cannot avoid. You may be thinking, all right, where do I start?

You start improving your ability to make decisions in exactly the same place you start any journey and with exactly the same resources. You decide. Start right where you are with whatever you've got. That is the cardinal principle of decision-making. DECIDE RIGHT WHERE YOU ARE WITH WHATEVER YOU'VE GOT. This is precisely why most people never master this important aspect of life. They permit their resources to dictate whether a decision will or can be made. When John Kennedy asked Werner Von Braun what it would take to build a rocket that would carry a man to the moon and return him safely to earth, his answer was simple and direct, 'The will to do it.' President Kennedy never asked if it was possible. He never asked if they could afford it or any one of a thousand other questions, all of which would have, at the time, been valid questions.

President Kennedy made a decision. He said the United States would put a man on the moon and return him safely to earth before the end of the decade (1960s). The fact that it had never been done before in all the hundreds of thousands of years of human history was not even a consideration. He DECIDED where he was with what he had. The objective was accomplished in his mind the second he made the decision. It was only a matter of time, which is governed by natural law, before the goal was manifested in the physical or material form for the whole world to see.

If you are content with the old world, try to preserve it,
it is very sick and cannot hold out much longer. But if

you cannot bear to live in everlasting dissonance between your beliefs and your life, thinking one thing and doing another, get out of the medieval whited sepulchers and face your fears. I know very well it is not easy.

–Leo Tolstoy

A few years ago a close friend, Marta, wanted to attend one of my mentor courses in the United States, which costs tens of thousands of dollars. At that time she was unable to touch her funds and had a very short time to make her decision. She came to me quite desperate and asked me to guide her through this.

I explained to her that money was not important until she decided what was it that she really wanted to do. 'Once you make the decision, the money will follow, and this will always happen. If that is the only benefit you receive from this message on decision making, then engrave it in the depth of your subconscious mind. This can change your life,' I said.

I later explained to Marta that I do not make any decision based on money (whether I can or can't afford it). The only thing that I focus on is whether it is something I want to do. We also talked about how the universe is unlimited and that whatever it is that she (or anybody else) wants, the universe will find a way to deliver it to her when the decision is firmly made. So Marta finally decided to go.

I am well aware that many people will say that this is absurd. You can't just decide to do something if you do not have the necessary resources. And that's fine if that is the way they choose to think. I see that as a very limiting way of thinking. In truth, it probably is not thinking at all. It is very likely an opinion being expressed that was inherited from another older member of the family who did not think either.

Later that week, while Marta was taking a nap, she was struck by an idea of how to raise money without touching her funds. She asked people around her to sponsor her trip. In return she would teach them what she had learnt. With that she managed to raise most of the money and completed the course.

There is nothing either good or bad,
but thinking makes it so.

–William Shakespeare

Thinking is very important. Decision makers are great thinkers. Do you ever consider your thoughts? How they affect the various aspects of your life? Although this should be one of our most serious considerations, unfortunately, for many people it is not. Only a select few attempt to control or govern their thoughts.

Anyone who has made a study of the great thinkers, the great decision makers, the achievers of history, will know they very rarely agreed on anything when it came to the study of human life. However, there was one point on which they were in complete and unanimous agreement: we become what we think about.

What do you think about? You and I must realize that our thoughts ultimately control every decision we make. You are the sum total of your thoughts. By taking charge this very minute, you can guarantee yourself a good day. Refuse to let unhappy, negative people or circumstances affect you.

The greatest stumbling block you will encounter when making important decisions in your life is circumstance. We let circumstances get us off the hook when we should be giving it everything we've got. More dreams are shattered and goals lost because of circumstance than any other single factor.

How often have you caught yourself saying, 'I would like to do or have this but I can't because…' Whatever follows **because** is the circumstance. Circumstances may cause a detour in your life, but you should never permit them to stop you from making important decisions.

It is simple maths. You are the sum total of your thoughts. By taking control of your thoughts this very instant, you can make or break your day.

Surround yourself with positive energy, and don't let other people spoil your day. In the end it is up to you whether your day is a good one or a bad one.

Circumstances - what are circumstances? I make circumstances.

–Napoleon

The next time you hear someone say they would like a holiday in Paris or to purchase a particular automobile but they can't because they have no money, explain they don't need the money until they have made a decision to go to Paris or purchase the car. When the decision is made, that person will figure out a way to get the amount needed. People always do.

Many misguided individuals try something once or twice and if they do not hit the bulls-eye, they feel they are a failure. Failing does not make anyone a failure, but quitting most certainly does, and quitting is a decision. By following that form of reasoning, you would have to say that when you make a decision to quit, you make a decision to fail.

When you're inventing, if you flunk 999 times and succeed once, you're in.

–Charles F. Kettering

The world remembers the great inventors for their inventions, not their failures. Name one of Benjamin Franklin's failed inventions. When all is said and done, you will be remembered for your achievements, not your failures.

Many years ago a deaf and blind Helen Keller was asked if she thought there was anything worse than being blind. She quickly replied that there was something much worse. She said, 'The most pathetic person in the world is a person who has their sight but no vision.' I agree with Helen Keller.

At 91 J. C. Penney was asked how his eyesight was. He replied that his sight was failing but his vision had never been better. That is really great, isn't it? When your vision is clear, all other things take a backseat. As long as you know what you want, you can obtain it, and it becomes easy to make decisions.

Take the first step in predicting your own prosperous future. Build a mental picture of exactly how you would like to live. Make a firm decision to hold on to that vision and positive ways to improve everything will begin to flow into your mind. It's amazing the opportunities that you do not see when you are not looking. Opportunities are all around you; you need only to look.

Many people get a beautiful vision of how they would like to live or what they would like from their business, but because they cannot see how they are going to make it happen, they let the vision go. If they knew how they were going to get it or do it, they would have a plan, not a vision. There is no inspiration in a plan, but there sure is in a vision. When you get the vision, freeze-frame it in your mind with a decision, and don't worry about how you will do it or where the resources will come from. Charge your decision with enthusiasm – that is important. Refuse to worry about how it will happen. There is a power in the universe much greater than you that never expresses itself other than perfectly. That always takes care of that responsibility.

There is no situation that isn't made worse by worry. Worry never solves anything. Worry never prevents anything. Worry never heals anything. Worry serves only one purpose: it makes matters worse.

If we worry, we don't trust; if we trust, we don't worry.
Worry does not empty tomorrow of its grief, but it does
empty today of its joy.

–James Kurtz

Worrying about lack is a clear indication there is a serious misunderstanding with respect to our source of supply. By our source, I mean you and me. We are both receiving every good that comes into our life from the same source. There is only one source of supply. That is Spirit. Everything comes from Spirit. When you clearly understand that, you will find making a decision easy to do.

When you truly understand the source of supply and then enhance your understanding with the law by which Spirit works, you will be able to make a decision and hold the picture of the successful outcome as a result of that decision knowing that Spirit will instantly begin sending to you whatever you require for the manifestation of your picture.

I am well aware that millions of people will laugh at you if you attempt to get them to accept what I am saying. However, it is important for you to remember those same people are not able to explain why they are rejecting it or why it cannot happen.

I found an interesting idea that you can gain tremendous benefits from in your efforts to become a more effective decision maker: advanced decision making. Isn't that great? Think about it. We make advanced bookings when we fly somewhere to eliminate any confusion or problems when time arrives for the journey. We do the same with renting a car for the same reason. Think of the problems you will eliminate by making many of the decisions you must make well in advance.

That same concept works with a person when on a diet to lose weight. Her decisions are made in advance. If she is offered a big slice of chocolate cake, she doesn't have to say gee, that looks good. I wonder if I should. The decision is made in advance.

I decided a long time ago that I would not participate in discussions of why something cannot be done. The only compensation you will ever receive for participating in or giving energy to that type of discussion is something you do not want. Why would you want to put yourself in an environment filled with negative energy? I always find it amazing at the number of seemingly intelligent people who persist in dragging you into these negative brainstorming sessions. In one breath these people tell you they seriously want to accomplish a particular objective. And, in the next breath, they begin talking about why they can't. If these people spent the same amount of time brainstorming about positive things, think of all the good things they could accomplish. Negative energy drives people to negative results, so why would you ever want to get caught up in negative energy?

Permit me to caution you. Advanced decisions must be mixed with an ample supply of discipline. All peak performers understand and use discipline. Any decision you make must be backed by discipline. Research indicates that highly successful individuals make decisions quickly and change those decisions slowly, if they are changed at all. By comparison the person who rarely enjoys any degree of success makes decisions slowly and changes decisions quickly and often. Once you believe in something, get behind it and stick to your guns.

Those individuals who rarely win generally have the habit of being influenced in their decision making by the opinions of others while their successful counterparts follow their own counsel. The most natural thing in the world for you to do in life is probably the most destructive in so far as succeeding at anything is concerned, that is following the crowd. Historically, the crowd has always been travelling in the wrong direction.

You were encouraged to be like the other kids when you were young. You have been conditioned to follow the crowd. In school you even dressed like the other kids. Well, you're not a child any longer, and you're not like the other kids. You are unique.

Chapter 9

Never Go Solo

Get Coaching

Would you like your life to massively improve? Do you seek a higher level of success? Did you know that your potential is up to 1000 times greater than the biggest goal you can imagine right now?

A long time ago, I was struggling in my life. I had no goals, no dreams and no ambition. Success in any area of my life seemed impossible. And then it all changed; I met a mentor. You can get only so far on your own. Successful people don't become successful by themselves.

Mentors and role models are both people you admire and appreciate. The main difference between the two is that role models are people you admire and appreciate from a distance. While you may deeply appreciate the ability of your favourite movie star or your number one author, you probably won't be able to pick up the phone and chat with either one of them.

Mentors, on the contrary, are 'up close and personal.' They are people you have a personal relationship with. They can brighten up your desolate day with their positivity, suggest a new perspective that you might have failed to notice or empathize when something doesn't turn out the way you had hoped it would. Mentors offer guidance, encouragement and friendship.

Having a mentor means that you have someone you can communicate with on a regular basis and can learn from and lean on. And both of you will benefit from the relationship.

Mentors are there not only to help you pinpoint a career pathway or encourage and assist you with assignments but also to listen to you and perhaps share their own life experiences with you so that you can make better decisions.

Mentors can help you in many different ways. They show you different aspects of the world, often indirectly guiding you to careers that you might never have considered before. They teach you the skills that you need, from how to study a book to applying the principles of it in your life. They listen to you talk it out as you struggle with the serious and not so serious life issues you face, and then they give you their thoughts and advice from the perspective of someone who has been there.

Of course, mentors cannot fix all your issues, find you the perfect job or know every answer to every question. They can, however, open doors and point out new pathways. They are there to support you when things don't work out and celebrate with you when they do.

I know that there is a good possibility that you do not have a mentor at this point and that you are not even thinking about entering into such a commitment yet. Many athletes, actors and business leaders all have mentors or had some form of mentoring in their life; so why not you?

Benefits of Engaging in a Mentoring Program

You will learn self-accountability: You may realize that just the thought of your mentors would push you to look into some of your important pending matters without their having to say anything. I always find myself acting on some of the things that I promised to do so that when my mentors do ask me, I am ready to answer them with a good statement. The relationship in a way has built-in accountability.

Your mentors will be people you look up to, and you will want them to think positively of you. When you don't accomplish a goal or you fall back on old habits, you won't be just letting yourself down; you will also be letting down your mentors.

I know people who will go out of their way for a friend or a family member but will procrastinate when it comes to their own life. These people lack self-confidence. But when someone you look up to believes in you, you will believe in yourself and have more confidence to move forwards in your own life.

Mentors will probably ask you questions that you may never ask yourself: Sometimes you may postpone answering some questions just because you can. You will do this even for questions when you know the answers are not good. By postponing the asking of the hard questions, you are not solving any problem; you are just avoiding the short-term sorrow. Your mentor may not be so nice to you. He will have no problem whatsoever asking those hard questions and actually prompting you to start doing something about those questions. Your mentor will also give you the boost that you may sometimes need to face your issues.

Your mentor will be someone who is willing to push you forwards, even if that means putting you in awkward situations that you would want to avoid. Remember what avoiding these situations has gotten you. Know that your mentor has your best intentions in mind when he makes you ask the uncomfortable questions that you may not want to seek answers to.

Too many of us live our lives avoiding the most important questions in life. That isn't living. That is living life like a fugitive. Face the tough questions head on. It may take some time to answer them, but when you do, your life will begin to move forwards at a rapid pace. With the tough questions taken care of, the easy ones will seem easier than they once did because you will have the confidence to tackle all questions thrown your way.

You can learn to reflect: A mentor has got no other plan but to help you get the most out of yourself. So you never have to worry about any other side effects as you discuss your life and work-related issues. That in itself will let you open up and reflect on things at a level that you have never seen before. You can rest assured that your mentor has got your true interest at heart.

Look at all the aspects of your life and reflect on them. Why are things in your life the way they are? What paths have you traversed to put you where you are in life at this moment? Reflecting on your past will help you move forwards in the future.

You can get help finding out what the real problem is and work on it: Sometimes we keep messing with symptoms rather than attacking the real problems. I have found time and again that I discuss a particular problem with my mentor and actually we end up solving the real problem. Solving the real problem will in turn solve the symptomatic problems that you first set out to solve.

Reflecting on your past will help you find these problems. Do your reflecting alone or while meditating; then discuss what you have thought about with your mentor. In this way you can attack the real problem from all directions.

Many times our problems are masked by other smaller ones. By talking them over, you can dust away the small problems to unmask the larger ones that are buried beneath them.

You may escape from short-term achievement: Living the type of modern life that the masses do, it is so easy to just focus on the short-term goals and lose sight of what you really want in the long run. Although short-term achievements are great, accomplishments in the long run are even better. This is where having a mentor is beneficial. A mentor will not only help you achieve short term success but also keep you on track to achieving your long-term goals.

Think delayed gratification. Short-term goals are important and may make you feel great, but they can also get in the way of your future. To achieve everything you dream of, you may have to put aside some short-term satisfaction so that you can obtain something in the future.

You can get help getting into the thinking habit: Every hour I spend with my mentors, my thinking skyrockets. Most often people get carried away and practice 'thinking on the go' – meaning people think while they are engaged in doing something else. Mentoring will put a stop to that and teach you the art of thinking properly. I am sure none of us will argue on the importance of the need to think.

If half of your mind is somewhere else, then you will get only 50 per cent out of yourself to think about your life. But if you sit down and focus 100 per cent on the question, then you can get 100 per cent out of yourself. The more you put in, the more you take out.

You'll learn to welcome new possibilities: Your mentor will look at how you can improve your strengths. It is very rare that you are aware of the full potential of your strengths. Even if you are, you may not be making the most of them. A mentor works with you to certify that you are spending most of your time in the areas of your strengths and taking care of other things (where you are not that good) by putting a suitable structure in place.

You'll learn to be in harmony: You cannot do right in one field of life as long as you are busy doing wrong in any other field. Chances are that you may be neglecting several other parts of your life.

You would never drive a car with a missing wheel. When you live your life with certain aspects of it in shambles, you may as well be riding a bicycle without a chain or brakes. You cannot get proper performance out of yourself unless every part of your life, mental and physical, is in tiptop condition.

With your mentor's help, you can be assured of living a more harmonious life while enjoying success.

Mastermind

What Is a Mastermind Group?

A mastermind group is generally a small group of like-minded people who meet regularly to support each other's growth. The group members may have similar or different goals. The common denominator is that each member of the group accepts responsibility for supporting, advising and challenging other members in pursuit of their goals.

Why Gather?

When people get together and begin discussing their lives, powerful stuff takes place. It is the power of the mastermind group! And I recommend that everyone be involved with at least three to ten other people with whom they can share their hopes, dreams, successes and struggles.

We get a great deal of clarity when we receive input from others who are not as close to our situation. And we are empowered as we pour good stuff into others who are seeking input and direction for their lives.

According to Napoleon Hill, the mastermind can be defined as 'coordination of knowledge and effort, in a spirit of harmony, between two or more people, for the attainment of a definite purpose.'

When I first began my seemingly endless search for the right answer to grow in life, it seemed as if there were obstacles at every corner. I was troubled by indecision, procrastination, fear of taking risks, lack of money and lack of knowledge. Being alone day in and day out allowed me to create all kinds of bad thoughts in my head. I didn't interact with people who were going through the same type of things that I was, until I found a mastermind group.

The idea of masterminding has been around for hundreds of years and has long been touted as one of the best ways to see rapid success in your life. Why? Because the collective knowledge, expertise, ideas and encouragement of the many is far more powerful than the mind of one.

Benefits of a Mastermind Group

Specialized knowledge: Nobody knows it all, which is one of the common reasons why people fall short of their goal or choose not to take chances. People believe they don't have the knowledge or required education to get where they want to be. The fact is no successful individual has become successful because she knew everything. Napoleon Hill talks about this at great length in Think and Grow Rich in the chapter 'Specialized Knowledge.' The most successful people are not the ones who know everything but who know how to get people to do for them what they don't know. In a mastermind group, people are able to leverage the knowledge and strengths of everyone around them to move forwards more quickly towards their own goals.

Definiteness of purpose: Definiteness of purpose is a key to your success. If you do not know with absolute certainty what you want, you will never reach the level of success that you want. Mastermind groups offer knowledge, information and direction. The members of a mastermind group help you stay on track, help you with things that you are supposed to be doing for your growth and generally serve as a more rational voice inside you to keep your mind focused on your goals. Do not underestimate the power of this.

Infinite experience: An individual who is trying to develop a strategy to grow his business for the first time has a high probability of failure because he has finite experience. He has only what he currently knows to guide him. However, the mastermind group has infinite experience. It has years of combined experience, knowledge and insight you can draw from to accelerate your learning curve.

You don't hire a person to build an entire house. Someone pours the foundation; the framers build the walls; the plumber lays the pipe; every aspect of the home is accomplished by an expert. If you really wanted to know how a house was built, you wouldn't just ask a framer. You would put all the people together who take part in the house's construction and pick all of their brains. You do the same when you are trying to rebuild your life.

Group energy: Many entrepreneurs struggle because they don't have consistent daily interaction with their peers. They may work with clients and attend events a few times a month, but working in isolation can be dangerous. Having a mastermind group that you are part of weekly can keep you connected, help you to see that your struggles are not unique and that you can have outrageous success even if you stumble once in a while. Mastermind groups keep us honest and on track and encourage us to do more and be more.

Invest in Yourself

Books, Home Audio Courses and Seminars

How many of you would attend a motivational seminar or buy a book on self-development or a home audio course to grow in life? I am asking because I know quite a few people who are either intimidated by the idea or are a little embarrassed. As a matter of fact, I have friends who are afraid to purchase a self-help book in fear of what others may think. There is absolutely no shame in trying to improve yourself. Although self-improvement is a very personal matter, here are some reasons why you should go out of your way to buy books or audio programs and study at home or attend a motivational seminar.

Help from books and audio programs: From books you can learn to use your imagination and creativity to inspire yourself. A great idea, if applied, can completely change your life. Also, books can be taken with you anywhere you go.

An audio program can be repeated as many times as possible until you have gained complete understanding of the content. Also, repetition is an important ingredient to learning. Like a book, an audio program will show you a different perspective each time you listen to it. With time, if the audio course is studied regularly, you will notice a significant improvement in your level of awareness.

Energy and atmosphere: The energy confined within a seminar is extraordinary. You will not find another event like it. It is quite an experience, in terms of excitement and enthusiasm, for both the presenter and the audience. This positivity is addictive, and you always find yourself having a good time. Although the topics and stories may sometimes be serious, the atmosphere is never one of sadness or sorrow. It is about re-inventing yourself and making your life better. Put together hundreds or thousands of like-minded people and you get pure magic. The mere vibration that flows through the event will leave you wanting more.

Networking: Seminars are some of the best places to make contacts with like-minded people, which can develop into fruitful business relationships or long-lasting friendships. If you run your own business, this is a wonderful opportunity to network and get the word out about your company, as well as learn about others in your region whom you may not have been aware of. Everyone who attends seminars usually leaves with a few new friends. Having friends and contacts on the same level as you are is extremely important to help you succeed.

New insights: In a seminar the presenter can go deeper into the book or the audio course that made you want to attend the seminar in the first place. Therefore, you are likely to get much more information and insights into what helped the presenter create specific material. It also helps to humanize the author, and when you see that the life-changing knowledge that you read or listened to was created by a human being not that much different from you, it will show you that you are just as capable of creating wonderful things in your life as well. In addition, these seminars usually include guest speakers, so you are likely to get more knowledge from different points of view. Also, you will be able to learn about some new authors or new courses that you were not aware of previously. You definitely leave a motivational seminar with tonnes of new knowledge.

Inspiring stories: One of my favourite aspects of motivational seminars is that they are interactive with the audience. People are encouraged to ask questions and share their stories. It's one thing to hear about the presenters and their stories about turning their lives around, but when you hear it from someone sitting next to you, to me that is even more powerful. It makes everything real and possible for you, in that if these people next to you are capable of it, then nothing is stopping you from doing the same. In addition, this is a time for you to share your success story too! A great thing about this type of event is that everyone is there to help each other.

Commitment: Attending a motivational seminar requires quite an investment from you. It can be quite expensive in terms of money and time. Most seminars are many hours long, some stretching over two or three days. Also, you need to attend with your utmost focus and concentration, along with an open mind, so that you can absorb the information and experience properly. You can clearly see that it requires a vast dedication on your part to effectively attend such an event. This is why so many people go home completely different individuals. When you combine such dedication with insightful knowledge, the result can truly be life changing.

Chapter 10

Action

Action is a great word, isn't it? Action, what do you think of when you hear the word? It has many uses and many connotations. If you were thinking of words that were motivational, action would have to be up near the top of the list. In the lines to follow, I want to show you some of the different meanings to this power word for your benefit.

In a movie or play, you will hear the director calling for action. The cameras begin to roll, and things begin to happen. Used in the context of war, action can have a very negative sting. You frequently hear of individuals being wounded or killed in action. Work is also described by actions: shovelling, typing, running, whatever the word, something is always getting done.

In this book, action is being used as a very positive power principle. I want the concept of action to play a positive role in your life. My Webster's dictionary has a number of different meanings for the word action. 'The process of doing' is the definition on which most people would focus their attention. Whenever you work towards a goal, you must complete some action to accomplish it.

I want to suggest you put a different twist on the word action. Make it a principle which gives you power. Make a decision to develop a reputation of a person of outrageous action, a person who makes the important moves, a person who gets the big things done.

When you want to go on holiday, make it worthwhile. Go around the world. Explore a country and visit a culture on the other side of the globe. Make the trip a memorable one. If the action is to improve your business, double or possibly triple your business. When you call for action, make it explosive action so that the big moves are not something in which other people are always involved. You become one of those other people.

Goethe, the German philosopher, has been quoted as saying, 'Before you can do something, you must first be something.' And, of course, Goethe was right. Before you paint a picture, you must first equip yourself as a painter. You must be a painter before you can apply the paint to the canvas. Doing is the expression of what has already taken place mentally. It is the expression of an impression. Action and doing are synonymous when they are used in this context. However, the word **action** adds an explosive dimension to the process of doing.

Think about it for a moment. If I had titled this chapter 'Doing,' it would have sounded weak when compared to 'Action.' **Action** is a power word. Doing sounds forced like, I have to do something. When you move into action on an idea, you are involved in the final stages of creation, insofar as that idea is concerned. Action is not something that should be focused on or forced. Action should be automatic. Keep that in mind!

Predators take action. Once you have found your vision and decided how you will complete that vision, you move into action. The predator sees its prey; it doesn't think. It moves instinctively, automatically. Action is something that is part of you but also part of a higher activity. You control the action as you control the arrow fired from a bow. You can aim the bow, you can steady the bow, but once you release the arrow, you have done all you can. The rest of the action takes place on its own.

Think of writing an essay or a letter. You may prepare what you are going to say, do some research or read over what others have said about an idea. Once you get all the necessary materials ready to write your essay, you begin. This is the action. All the research you have done begins to fall together. Sometimes things happen in your paper that you didn't even know you were going to do. This is an example of action taking over. If you prepare well enough, outside forces will come together to help you complete what it is that you set out to do.

The late Earl Nightingale said, 'Ideas are like slippery fish; if you don't gaff them with the point of a pencil, they will probably get away and may or might never come back.' That is a beautiful truth, worthy of serious consideration.

You learn many lessons as you gain experience living on this earth. One thing I have learned is that, as people, we are far too regimented in our behaviour.

Here is another point you might want to consider. When the time arrives for the birth to take place, the only people the mother wants in her life at that particular time are those people who are capable, competent and who want to give their undivided attention to assisting in the birth of her child. Long after the child has been safely delivered and Mum is completely rested from her flurry or creative activity, a little idle chatter with a few non-productive, possibly scatterbrained acquaintances or relatives would probably be allowed. Even then almost everyone's attention is attracted by magnificence of the newly arrived creation. New creation generally attracts almost everyone's attention and admiration. The supreme satisfaction, which many people miss out on in life, comes only to those main contributors who work in harmony with the Creator for the physical manifestation of the new creation. I have always felt that a mother receives a degree of satisfaction, which the father will never completely understand, as her contribution in the birth of the child is so much greater than that of the father's.

Now let's move back to the explosive word **action**. You want to be recognized as a person of action. I'm sure you do. You are a creative expression of life. You have been endowed with the mental tools that enable you to work in harmony with the ever present, all-powerful, all knowing Creator. So far as we know, you are the only form of life which has been given these marvellous mental powers. The nucleus of your being is creative; it is perfect. It is always longing for expansion and fuller expression. You are capable of and designed to do great work. You were never meant to spend your days involved in idle chatter or meaningless activity. It is your responsibility to grow, to develop a greater awareness, to enjoy every good imagined. If you haven't already got a dynamite idea running around your mind, adding dimensions of joy and enthusiasm to your days, quit whatever you are doing, lay back, relax and permit your imagination to move freely. Begin to look from within to your source of unlimited supply. Look at your work. How can you improve what you are doing? How can you make it 10 times, even 50 times better? Don't worry about getting paid for it; that will come. It must come. That is the law. Write your ideas down as they come to you before they leave your head.

ACTION IS THE EXPRESSION OF AN IMPRESSION.

WHEN YOU MENTALLY WORK ON YOUR BIG IDEAS,

THE ACTION BECOMES AUTOMATIC.

YOU WILL NOT BE ABLE TO STOP IT.

When you are mentally pregnant with a big idea, keep this idea in mind. Action comes when the idea is ready, not when the clock dictates. Have you ever noticed that the real professionals in every walk of life are not clock watchers? Nor are they controlled or guided by the dictates of the masses. When they are ready for action, they act.

The birth of ideas and the birth of babies are governed by exactly the same laws. Examine what I have just shared with you. Think, really think. There is only one all-knowing, creative power in this universe. This power expresses itself in many ways, but it always works the same way, by law. Every form of creation is by law.

When a woman is carrying a baby in her womb, she is referred to as being pregnant with a new child. To make certain she carries the baby to full term and a healthy birth, certain rules must be followed. Rest, relaxation, physical exercise, freedom from worry or stress, proper diet and nutrition are all considerations to which a responsible mother gives high priority. Let's keep this basic truth in mind: when the time for the birth of the baby arrives, nothing, absolutely nothing, but the birth receives Mum's attention. I should probably add complete and undivided attention. You just try to get her to go back to sleep or watch TV. You know how successful you would be.

Neither conditions nor circumstances should prevent you from creating and acting on your creations. Remember that action is the final stage of creation. The creation and action is continuous; it keeps going. So you should take the same precautions with your ideas. When you are creating and acting on your visions, nothing else should matter. Nurture your ideas, and give them every chance to succeed. If you do this, you will have a greater chance at success when you put your ideas into action.

Positive action is preceded by emotional involvement. Building the image and thinking about it continually gives it the energy it requires to sustain life. You are probably aware that millions of ideas either are aborted before birth or are stillborn. Negative suggestions from ignorant but well-meaning people coupled with doubt, worry and possibly envy generally take the life out of most great ideas. Just as the expectant mother must care for the unborn child she carries, you must care for the unborn idea you carry. Associate with positive-thinking people.

Henry David Thoreau told us that when he said, 'If a person will move confidently in the direction of their dream… and endeavour to live the life they have imagined… they will meet with success unexpected in common hours.' Thoreau was right. Mentally look after the idea, and one day it will just happen.

Action is the expression of an impression. When you mentally work on your big ideas, the action becomes automatic. You will not be able to stop it. The action comes through you, which causes reaction. The reaction comes from the universe. The action meeting the reaction alters your conditions, circumstances and environment that produce your result, your creation.

Permit me to share a wonderful story with you. It's a true story that happened to some very nice people in northern Ontario, Canada. The story is about a dirt-poor prospector who, day after day, month after month, year after year, would leave his home and his family to go prospecting for gold. There were times when they had next to nothing to eat. Whenever this man's wife or son voiced concern about the future, the man would assure them they need not worry; they had wonderful times coming when he found his gold mine. He was a man of great faith, but he was also a man of action. He imagined himself with a gold mine, and he would continually move into action out looking for it. He was a prospector.

> EVERY MOVEMENT IN WHICH YOU ENGAGE IS AN ACTION. ACTION IS SOMETHING IN WHICH YOU ARE ALREADY INVOLVED. THE TRICK IN LIFE IS TO CONTROL AND DIRECT THE ACTION, WHICH WILL EVENTUALLY CAUSE YOU TO FIND YOUR GOLD MINE.

It was the week between Christmas and New Year's Day. At that time of year in northern Ontario in Canada, the snow is several feet deep, and it is bitterly cold. The prospector lived in a predominantly Christian community, so being Christmas, very few people worked. Most folks lay around at home. It was a time to be with the family. Although I have not checked this out, I feel fairly safe in saying there were babies born that week in that cold, snow-swept town. The babies didn't care what the occasion was or what the weather was like; the time had elapsed and the babies arrived; mums gave birth.

Well, the time also arrived for this man's idea to be acted upon. No one prospected for gold in this area between Christmas and New Year's Day. Anyone who did or even suggested they would, were considered insane. Nevertheless, this poor prospector called his partner and said, 'It's time; we must go.' Something inside of him caused him to move into action. So off they went, just outside of town. The snow was so deep they were able to venture only a few feet off the main highway. Standing a few feet off the main road in freezing temperatures and deep snow, the poor prospector said, 'This is the place.' They went far beyond what any right-minded gold prospector would consider suitable with their drilling. However, it was at that very place between Christmas and New Year's Day that the poor prospector and his partner became extremely wealthy, multi-million dollar owners of the Hemlow Gold Mines.

It was at dinner party one evening that Paul Larch told this story. You see, the poor prospector who became the wealthy owner of the Hemlow Gold Mines is John Larch, Paul's father. Paul just knew his dad would find a gold mine. He knew it because his dad kept telling him he would, from the time he was a little boy. And as Paul said, 'Dad believed he would.' That belief over the years fuelled the idea, the image. John Larch impressed such great energy upon his subconscious mind for so long, he moved himself into the vibration he had to be in to attract what he attracted. The image within John Larch became so explosive it had to be acted upon. Christmas, cold, snow, none of that mattered. He had to move into action on the idea. The action was automatic. It was the expression of the impression.

Do you have an idea big enough to keep you enthusiastic for years? John Larch did. A benefit that came to John as a result of the gold mine is the faith he instilled in his son Paul, the 'can-do' attitude with which Paul was raised. John Larch was a very rich man before he ever struck gold. He had and gave his son what no amount of gold could ever buy.

Adjust your thinking. If it is on the wrong track, fix it. Remember this: what you don't fix, your children will inherit.

It is easy for a person to fall into the trap of thinking that great things can happen only to others and never to themselves. If you are caught in this trap, I suggest that you analyze the creative process. You will see that you have the tools for greatness. I have personally been studying the lives of successful people for more than 20 years. Although these people came from varied backgrounds, there is one factor which remained constant, and that was the creative process which produced the results in their lives. Their results were preceded by an action, which was automatic. The expression of the thought and ideas had been impressed upon their emotional mind over time. They became what they thought about. The thought always propels action.

You see, the bottom lines are obvious when you really think about it. That is what all the big producers do. You are like the great people you read about. Take action, go and meet them. The more of these people you get to know, the more you will see that you are like them and the better you will feel about yourself. The better you feel about yourself, the more confident you will become. The more confident you become, the easier it will be for you to move into action on your big ideas and to solve the inherent problems that come with them.

When we feel confident about ourselves, we know we can solve the problems or at least put them into perspective and remind ourselves of our abilities when things aren't going well. Don't worry about what might happen when you explode into action on your big idea. Whatever happens will be what must happen for your idea to move into its final form of creation, the physical form, which is always your result.

Chapter 11

Meditation

Meditation brings wisdom; lack of mediation leaves ignorance. Know well what leads you forward and what holds you back and choose the path that leads to wisdom.

–Shakyamuni Buddha

Millions of people around the world go through their entire lives frustrated with the way they are living. Many steps can help you achieve success. It takes a lot of energy to constantly work on yourself all day every day, and sooner or later your body will need to reboot. Meditation is a great tool not only to help regain balance in your life but also to open your mind to different ways of looking at the world.

If you answer yes to one or more of these scenarios, learning meditation techniques may be right for you.

Do you

- Often feel broken, empty, unsupported, unloved, powerless and distressed?

- Seem to fall short and get stuck in comfort zones no matter how hard you try to break free?

- Attempt to get validation and support from people who don't validate and support you?

- Feel controlled by your environment and other people?

- Struggle to create your truth and detach from the negativity and limiting factors surrounding you?

- Know that your life is supposed to be more than it is yet can't find the way through?

- Often replay painful patterns that you know aren't serving you?

- Hang on to painful situations and people even though you know it hurts?

- Feel guilty when you try to say no?

- Fail to stand up for yourself because you fear criticism, rejection or abandonment?

By using meditative techniques to help you understand, you will be able to break free from dependency and live the life you choose to experience. This is true personal freedom.

Bruce Lee once said, 'Empty your mind; be formless, shapeless, like water. Now you put water into a cup, it becomes the cup. You put water into a bottle, it becomes the bottle. You put it in a teapot and it becomes the teapot. Now water can flow or it can crash. Be water, my friend!'

Lee's metaphor comparing the mind to water is brilliant. Think of this statement. If your mind is like water, it can take on any form it needs to. You can therefore shape your mind to whatever situation you find yourself in. If you are not living the life you want, it is because you have chosen to shape your mind into living this life. Through meditative processes you empty your body of everything. Then you can shape your body into whatever shape you choose, whatever life you choose, and your mind will fill this shape and allow you to live how you want to live.

You may be thinking that this process takes years and years to learn. Wrong. Believe me, I know it sounds very confusing, but after you have read this chapter, you can begin to meditate as soon as today!

You are never alone or helpless. The force that guides the stars guides you too.

–Shrii Shrii Anandamurt

Dictionary.com defines meditation as 'continued or extended thought; reflection; contemplation.' When you think of meditation, what do you imagine? A guru sitting cross-legged, palms up while making humming noises? Movies and media have turned meditation into a process practiced by Eastern cultures and those involved in martial arts: a process where a seeker spends years in the mountains of Tibet or some other far off mystical land and hums his way into enlightenment. The truth is that many people on every continent use meditation to live a better life. When you think of the word meditation, think of relaxation, a sort of conscious relaxation.

Many of us have practiced a certain level of meditation without even knowing it. When was the last time you experienced a stressful event that caused your anxiety levels to skyrocket into space? Taking tests, meeting deadlines, paying bills or going to the doctor can send people over the edge. How did you try to calm yourself during these episodes? When life seems to be too much we often say stop and take a deep breath or slowly count to ten. Both of these techniques are basic meditation. When you focus all your energies on your breathing, your mind slowly forgets about the cause of your anxiety. Meditation takes practice, but with repeated effort, you can completely clear your mind and think of nothing. This is when true meditation occurs. You will achieve complete peace and calmness and even open your mind to new personal insights regarding your life.

We could say that meditation doesn't have a reason or doesn't have a purpose. In this respect it's unlike almost

*all other things we do except perhaps making music and
dancing. When we make music we don't do it in order to
reach a certain point, such as the end of the composition.
If that were the purpose of music then obviously the
fastest players would be the best. Also, when we are
dancing we are not aiming to arrive at a particular place
on the floor as in a journey. When we dance, the journey
itself is the point, as when we play music the playing
itself is the point. And exactly the same thing is true in
meditation. Meditation is the discovery that the point of
life is always arrived at in the immediate moment.*

–Alan Watts

In our twenty-first century world, life is fast and hectic. The stresses we all face can be overwhelming. Some of us can deal with stress and some actually thrive on stress, but for many stress leads to anxiety attacks, which can actually cripple and cause severe mental problems. Our mind can tolerate only so much stress, and when our mind goes, our body follows. Pills with names spanning the English alphabet claim to cure every sort of stress-related illness, but pills only block the pain; they don't fix the source of the pain. Everything you need to cure your mind is stored in your mind. Everything you need in life is already inside you. You need only to find the key to open the vault in which all this power is hidden. For many meditation is the key.

I would like to share a story with you about a woman named Tara. Tara married young and chose to have children and begin her family instead of attending university. Tara had two children, both girls, and spent her time working a job she didn't enjoy so that her girls could have all the things she couldn't growing up.

For 20 years Tara was a secretary for a law firm. She spent her days answering phones and scheduling appointments for her boss. She was very close with her girls, and they often shared their dreams with each other. Susan, the oldest, wanted to go to school to be a veterinarian. Jaime, the youngest, was a free spirit and wanted to move to Los Angeles to pursue acting.

One day the girls asked their mother, 'Mom, what did you want to be when you were a girl.'

Tara answered, 'I always wanted to be a mother.'

'Well,' they said, 'if you were never a mother, what would you have done?'

Tara thought for a bit. As her old childhood dreams flooded into her mind, a smile crept across her face. 'I guess I always wanted to be a reporter, a writer for a newspaper.'

Tara and her girls talked about this idea. Susan and Jaime thought their mother should chase her dream, but in Tara's mind she was too old. She was in her mid 40s. How could she do something like that? Her children were young and had all the time in the world to chase their dreams. Tara believed that she had sacrificed her dreams so that her children could live the lives they wanted.

This struck Susan and Jaime, and they decided to do something to help their mother. She had done so much for them; they felt that it was their turn to help. After school one day, Jaime overheard her teacher talking to a colleague about meditation. He said that it had changed his life and helped him move in a direction he had always wanted to take, but he was too scared to begin. Jaime approached this teacher and told him about how her mother's 'friend' was going through some tough times. Her teacher told her to look into the process of meditation.

After doing some research, the sisters decided to talk to Tara about the process. Tara was sceptical at first, but at the insistence of her daughters decided to give it a try. 'If not for myself,' she thought, 'I'll do it for my girls.'

The journey to recovery is never the same for any two individuals. For those who truly want to recover and live better lives, it can be as fast as flipping a light switch. Those who still flirt with old bad habits will have a longer trip to recovery.

Within one week Tara began meditating every day. Meditation opened up a new world for Tara, a personal world where she was able to see who she was and what she really wanted out of life. Once she found her calling, she grabbed hold of it and enrolled in a two-year journalism school. After completing the two years, she found a job working for a small newspaper in her hometown.

Meditation is not just a tool; it is a weapon. You may not know what you want out of life, but you know that you need to change. Use meditation to find out who you are and what you want. After you have found it, don't procrastinate, but take hold and never let go.

The Process

How do you begin meditating? Like everything else in this life, you just begin. But since your mind needs to be completely clear of clutter to achieve the proper level of relaxation, a few items help to assist the beginner in meditation.

Wear comfortable loose clothing. Loose clothes aren't worn because they are hip in the meditating community; they are worn because they are comfortable and allow the body the freedom to take deep breaths without restriction.

Find a place were you can completely relax, and make this your designated meditating area. A comfortable, quiet area where you are not distracted is key when meditating. Many people believe that being outdoors surrounded by nature helps while others meditate indoors in the comfort of their own home. Find the place that works for you, and keep coming back to this place.

Rituals are important in meditation. If you need to light candles, burn incense or listen to soft relaxing music, do so. After a time, your mind will instinctively know that you are beginning the process of meditation and will instinctively calm itself.

Although it is possible to meditate in many different positions, begin by sitting. Sit in a position that is comfortable and allows you to easily and comfortably breathe deeply. With your eyes partially closed, begin to breathe in deeply and focus on the passage of air into your body and lungs. When you exhale, do so softly and feel the air leaving your body. Continue this process for five to ten minutes, however long feels comfortable for you. For the optimal benefits of this process, try to meditate once a day. As you become more confident with the meditation process, you may want to meditate twice a day or for longer intervals.

The mind is the most powerful tool at the body's disposal. Meditation helps exercise the mind. After you have become proficient in meditation techniques, you will be able to use your mind to help certain parts of your body. When your mind focuses on a particular part of the body, the blood flow to that region of the body increases causing cells in that area to receive more oxygen and nutrients.

Meditation helps the mind concentrate. When the mind is trained in concentration, stressful situations can be easily overcome. When we are overwhelmed, the stress of the situation can cause us to lose sight of our goals and fail at the project at hand. When you have trained your mind to concentrate, you can block out all the stress surrounding you and focus on the task.

Meditation also has many health benefits, including the following:

- Lowering oxygen consumption

- Decreasing repertory rates

- Increasing blood flow and lowering the heart rate

- Increasing exercise tolerance in heart patients

- Leading to a deeper level of relaxation

- Bringing the blood pressure to normal levels

- Reducing anxiety attacks by lowering the levels of blood lactate

- Decreasing muscle tension

- Reducing headaches

- Building self-confidence

- Reducing pre-menstrual syndrome

Meditation is a powerful process that can help you turn your life around. Its mental, physical and medical benefits have been known for centuries but are only recently being understood. Learn the process and focus your energies and you can achieve anything you put your mind to. Turn your mind into water and fill the container of your dreams.

When you meditate you have to try to quiet and calm the mind. There should be no thought within the mind. Right now you feel that if you can cherish twenty ideas at a time, then you are the wisest man on earth. The more thoughts that enter into our minds, the cleverer we feel we are. But in the spiritual life it is not like that. If consciously we can make the mind calm and quiet, we feel that a new creation dawns inside us.

–Sri Chinmoy

Chapter 12

Persistence

*I know the price of success: dedication, hard work and an
unremitting devotion to the things you want
to see happen.*

–Frank Lloyd Wright

Life can be tough on a person. It can be tough on a family. So many people lack the mental ability to hang in there during the tough times. You can control your thoughts. You can practice perspective by changing the way you interpret your circumstance, situations and environments. The task is not to see a new world but to see the world with new eyes. The person who can change the way she views her world will win without fail.

John Milton said, as I mentioned before, 'The mind is its own place, and in itself can make a Heaven of Hell, a Hell of Heaven.' The thoughts that dominate your mind will control what happens in your life. You have the ability to control what occurs in your world.

A stranger chanced upon several workers in a small town in Italy. Curious and interested, he began to inquire from the workers as to what they were doing. 'I'm laying bricks,' said the first worker. After a few minutes of idle chat, he asked of another, 'What are you doing? Laying bricks, eh?' The other worker, somewhat indignantly responded with shoulders straight and firmness of voice, 'Laying bricks? No sir. I am building a cathedral.'

Both men were doing the same type of work, but their views were very different. One saw his job as monotonous while the other viewed his work as part of something bigger than the individual bricks. He saw what the bricks were going to become. Two people, two perspectives.

How come some people are able to make the best of any situation while others can only see the worst? When one person always looks at the bad in a situation and another always sees the good, who do you think will go further in life? Who do you think will succeed if both are presented with the same task? Optimism carries a person a long way.

Everyone meets obstacles. Everyone needs perspective in the face of those challenges. Your response to dealing with the storms of life will dictate the results you achieve. What follows are practical solutions to dealing with those times in life when everything seems to be going the opposite to your preferences.

In 1953 a beekeeper from Auckland, New Zealand, earned world recognition, with fame and fortune to follow. Knighted by Queen Elizabeth for his accomplishments, Sir Edmund Hillary and his native guide Tenzing Norgay became the first two people to climb Mount Everest and safely return, after having tried and failed on two previous attempts. Hillary had two obvious character strengths which literally took him to the very top: vision and persistence. Without persistence all his skills would have meant nothing. These qualities and characteristics are the same as those you need to lead you to the top of your mountain.

You are confronted by mountains every day. You can either climb the mountain or remain in the foothills. Any successful person will tell you that persistence is absolutely essential to climbing the mountains. The individuals who remain in the foothills have never chosen to develop this strength. These people dream of being stars, they want to receive the fame and fortune, but fame is not a common suitor. Fame comes calling only after a high price has been paid. The poor people who march in the foothills refuse to pay the price.

Napoleon Hill wrote in his book Think and Grow Rich: 'There may be no heroic connotation to the word persistence, but the character is to the quality of man what carbon is to steel.' Hill was right.

Persistence is a unique mental strength, a strength which is essential to combat the fierce power of the repeated rejections and numerous other obstacles that sit in waiting and are all part of winning in a fast-moving, ever-changing world. There are hundreds of biographies of highly successful men and women who have cut a path for others to follow while leaving their mark on the scrolls of history. Every one of these great individuals was persistent. In many cases it was the only quality that separated them from everyone else.

Consider Ben Hogan. He weighed only 135 pounds, but every ounce was saturated with persistence. Born into a poor family, Hogan began to caddie at a local golf club as a boy to earn extra money for his family. This led to the birth of a dream: he would become a great golfer. Through a great deal of hard work, practice and persistence, Hogan became one of the world's greatest golfers. In 1948 he won the U.S. Open Championship. His accomplishments earned him world recognition, but he had not yet faced his mountain.

The next year Hogan was involved in a head-on collision with a bus and he was not expected to survive his injuries. He did, but the doctors said he would never walk again. That was their opinion, not Hogan's! He insisted his golf clubs be put in the corner of the hospital room as he began to visualize himself playing golf again. One year later Hogan won the U.S. Open Championship again. The next year he won three major championships. In all, 54 of his victories followed that near-tragic accident. Does persistence pay? Ask Ben Hogan.

If you were to compare an entrepreneurial or sales career to one in the entertainment industry, you would find that every actor or actress holds a dream of becoming a star. Every entrepreneur or salesperson holds a similar dream. However, as an entrepreneur or as a salesperson you have much greater control over your destiny. No capricious director or casting agent can put a foot on the brake of your progress. You alone decide to quit or to continue when those inevitable mountains loom up on the road to your goal.

Every industry has its stars. There is always one person who stands out against the rest. It is estimated that 20 per cent of the salespeople take home 80 per cent of the commissions. You are the only one who can decide if you fit into that upper percentage or become part of the group that just ekes by.

And in the final analysis, as an entertainer, you must keep this beautiful truth firmly planted in your mind: even the capricious directors and casting agents of our world are always over-ruled by the laws of our universe. Whatever you conceive and believe, through persistence you must achieve.

Entrepreneurial situation or not, decide right now to be one of the people who makes it happen, to be part of the group that receives the lion's share of the profits.

Understand that to join this select group of big producers, you must begin your persistence exercises now. Make persistence your most well-developed mental muscle. Persistence cannot be replaced by any other quality. Superior skills will not make up for it. A well-rounded formal education cannot replace it nor will calculated plans or a magnetic personality. When you are persistent, you will become a leader in your industry. I picked up a piece of literature years ago which illustrates that point perfectly. Let me share it with you:

> *Nothing in the world can take the place of persistence....*
> *Talent will not; nothing is more common than*
> *unsuccessful people with talent.... Genius will not;*
> *unrewarded genius is almost a proverb. Education will*
> *not; the world is full of educated derelicts. Persistence*
> *and determination alone are omnipotent. The slogan*
> *'press on' has solved and always will solve, the problems*
> *of the human race.*

–Anonymous

The people who never tackle the mountains, who perpetually wander in the foothills most of their lives, have, in my opinion, lied to themselves and everyone else who would listen, so often and for so long, that they are no longer even aware of what they are doing. They say they are content with their results; they say that climbing the mountain is not important to them; they are getting by just fine the way they are. Odds are they secretly started to climb the mountain years ago and got scared. They hit the terror barrier, quickly retreated to their comfort zone and have been hiding behind their own false rationale ever since. They frequently justify their sick, mediocre performance with questions like why should I go all out? When I get there the boss will just want more. These poor non-productive individuals are lost or at best misguided. If you are not able to wake them up, make certain that you do not permit them to pull you into their trap. In fact, when you meet these poor souls, let them serve as a triggering mechanism to mentally double your commitment to yourself to become more persistent.

My Webster's dictionary has this to say about persistence: 'to continue, especially in spite of opposition or difficulties.'

To this point I have had quite a lot to say about persistence and those who have developed it and the necessity for persistence. But there is something missing in this message: how to. How do you become persistent? A good question.

Persistence is never developed by accident. You are not born with it. You cannot inherit it. No one in the entire world can develop persistence for you. Persistence is interwoven with success as the chicken is with the egg.

Ultimately persistence becomes a way of life, but that is not where it begins. To develop the mental strength, persistence, you must first want something. You have to want something so much that it becomes a heated desire, a passion in your belly. You must fall in love with the idea; yes, literally fall in love with the idea. Magnetize yourself to every part of the idea. Then persistence will be automatic.

The very idea of not persisting will become hateful, and anyone who even attempted to take your dream away from you or stop you or slow you down would be in serious trouble. Difficulties, obstacles, mountains will definitely appear on a regular basis, but, because of your persistence, they will be overcome by you every time.

All right, where does this leave you? It leaves you at the crossroads that every self-help book, every motivational CD, every seminar leads to. You must decide what you want, what you really want, way down deep inside or you will remain in the foothills surrounded by losers.

YOU ARE CONFRONTED BY THE MOUNTAINS EVERY DAY

YOU CAN EITHER CLIMB THE MOUNTAINS

OR REMAIN IN THE FOOTHILLS.

ANY SUCCESSFUL PERSON WILL TELL YOU THAT

PERSISTENCE IS ABSOLUTELY ESSENTIAL

TO CLIMB THE MOUNTAINS.

THE INDIVIDUALS WHO REMAIN IN THE

FOOTHILLS HAVE NEVER CHOSEN

TO DEVELOP THIS STRENGTH.

This is a subject I have studied all of my adult life, and I can tell you one thing I know for certain: very few people have admitted to themselves that this is what they want; this is what they really want and are prepared to give their life for it. That last statement may cause you to sit up and say wait a minute. And that's fine. But you should seriously think about it because you are already giving your life for what you are presently doing.

What are you doing? What are you trading your life for? Are you making a fair trade? Remember whatever you are doing was your decision. Or was it? You could possibly be one of those poor people who has been wondering in the foothills leaving the decisions of where they are going and what they are doing with their lives to other people. Just following, always following – that is where most people live.

If that is the case, that's okay. Don't let it bother you for one more valuable second of your life. Forgive yourself and that way of life. Let it go forever. Treat this message on persistence as your wake-up call!

This red-hot message on persistence will help you get out of the foothills and lead you to the very top of the mountain, all the way to the summit. It is not a chair lift; it will not make the climb any easier. You will still attract the necessary problems that come to strengthen you. But this message will definitely make the climb to the top of the mountain a lot more fun. It will also help you develop a granite-strong attitude, the certainty, the inner knowing that you will get to the top. The summit will be yours, and the view from the top will be awesome; it will be reward enough for all of the problems you encountered to get there.

Talking about the summits and persistence, let's go back and think about Edmund Hillary. What kind of a passion do you suppose he felt for his goal? He must have truly wanted to climb that mountain. Think of the physical and mental abuse he subjected himself to. He was obviously prepared to give his life for what he wanted. Every person who had ever seriously attempted to climb Everest as far back as our history records go, show that he either failed miserably or experienced a tragic death trying.

When most people think about Hillary and his expeditions, they ask what kept him going back year after year? He wanted – that is what kept him going, that is why he was persistent. He wanted. Really wanted. At a gut level, he wanted something enough to keep going.

People who not understand that usually ask why? Why did he want it? He didn't know why. He didn't have to know why! Why wasn't important. Want was important.

Hillary became the mountain climber. The whys in our life are blessings from Spirit. Let me repeat that. The whys in our life are blessings from Spirit. They are Spirit's way of turning us into a perfect instrument for Spirit to express itself through. Spirit is always for expansion and fuller expression. The essence of you is spiritual. Spirit is saying to your consciousness here, want this, really want it. When you want this enough, you will grow into the person who is capable of doing great work. You are worthy of having whatever you want. That is why ordinary people have always done extraordinary work. This is one of the greatest liberating truths you will ever hear.

Ordinary people have done extraordinary things because they consciously recognized what they wanted and refused to suppress or dismiss it. They would not let it go, even if failure, rejection, bankruptcy or death were starring them in the face. It would have had to be that way or ordinary people would never do the extraordinary. They would never persist. The power of their want and the intensity of their persistence caused them to draw on resources they previously were not aware they possessed. They expressed what they had within: greatness.

It's persistence, yes persistence

That expresses what you've got

It's persistence, yes persistence

That makes fame and fortune

Both so hot.

When the want is weak, you will quit at the first obstacle. The proper want is essential to persistence.

Come with me and as we review how Ben Hogan, a very ordinary young fellow, became such an absolutely extraordinary inspiration to millions of people. In one line the answer is obvious: he had a dream.

Every time I think of people like Hogan and Hillary and their dreams, I think of what another extraordinary man who has done the extraordinary said about situations like this.

If the dream is big enough, the facts don't count.

What started out as a dream for Ben Hogan quickly turned into an obsession. Hogan no longer had control of the dream; the dream was using him as an instrument to fulfil itself.

The great psychologist Alfred Adler, nailed it when he said, 'I am grateful to the idea that has used me.' I love it, I really do.

The very idea of persistence filled every cell of Hogan's being because his want was so strong. Remember, persistence is the real focus of this message. It is important that we keep that in mind because we could easily get lost climbing Mount Everest with Edmund Hillary or playing golf with Ben Hogan. They are not the stars of this movie; they are playing supporting roles. Persistence is the star. Properly digested in your mind, persistence will make you a star. It will give you that number one hit worldwide.

How does an idea, a want, a dream get such a grip on a person that persistence becomes a natural outgrowth of it? Napoleon Hill explained this very well when he said (I paraphrase) at first the idea (the want) has to be coaxed, nursed and enticed just to remain alive. But gradually the idea will take on a power of its own and will sweep aside all opposition. It will then coax, nurse and drive you.

He went on to explain that ideas have more power than the physical brains that gave birth to them. They have the power to live on long after the physical brain that created them has turned to dust. That is what happened to Hogan. He did not have much of a choice. Years before he had turned his will over to the idea of becoming the greatest golfer in the world. Nothing could shake Hogan loose from that idea. His entire mental being was directed towards doing whatever was required for that idea to move into physical form.

Have you decided what you want? Is your want that strong?

Come back to Hogan's history and you will understand better what I mean. Hogan was in a head-on collision in his car. He saw it coming and could not prevent it. His wife was in the front seat of the car with him. In an attempt to protect her, which he did, he threw himself in front of her. His body was crushed. The police who came to the scene thought he was dead.

There was debris all over the highway. The debris included his golf clubs, which were strewn all over the place. When they were putting Hogan into the ambulance, Mrs Hogan asked a police officer if he would please pick up Ben's golf clubs for her. The officer looked at her and replied, 'Lady, he is not going to need these sticks anymore.' Mrs Hogan looked at the policeman and told him that he obviously didn't know who they had just put in the ambulance.

When they got Hogan to the hospital, he was alive but not expected to live. The best doctors in the country were flown in to operate on him. It was their opinion that if he lived, he most certainly would never walk again. Hogan did live. He insisted that his golf clubs be placed in his hospital room where he could see them. He then demanded that an exercise bar be rigged up over his bed. This was in spite of the fact that he could not even move his arms, let alone lift his body. The hospital staff brought in the exercise bar just to humour him. They felt sorry for him. Negative facts versus wants, dreams, persistence – now you know what will win: the dream, of course, every time.

One year to the day of the accident, Hogan tied one of the greatest golfers who have ever played the game, Sam Snead, in a tournament. A tournament that many other golfers dropped out of because of driving rain. Hogan went on to write his name in the history books by winning 54 major tournaments after that accident.

Think of what persistence did for Hogan. It saved his life. It gave him life. Persistence will save your life. It will give you life.

If you are having trouble with persistence, your want is probably puny. It isn't big enough. That is probably the cause of your problem. Look around; it is a common problem; it is a human problem. Lack of persistence is almost always a symptom of the real problem. You must give these two concepts priority in your life: want and persistence.

Your life will be shallow if this is not given top priority. You will live like the minnows in the shallows. I want to entice you to come out here in the Deep Water of life. The view is spectacular. The people you meet are tremendous. They are all focused, dynamic, creative individuals. The energy is hot, hot, hot. Persistence will, as the lyrics of the song promise, cause you to 'express what you've got.' And when you do that, fame, which is not a common suitor, will most certainly have your number and will come calling. Fortune will be yours to hold. Oh, yes it will.

Nearly every man who develops an idea works at it up to the point where it looks impossible and then gets discouraged. That's not the place to become discouraged.

–Thomas Edison

I wonder if the people in the foothills would grasp the truth in that verse. You beat resistance with persistence. The poor people in the foothills have not learned that. Resistance keeps beating them, holding them back from what they truly want. They have not learned that they are the only problem they will ever have. Because of their quitting 'I-can't-do-it' attitude, they never move forwards and always let small obstacles keep them from their goals. Persistence turns wants into reality. Persistence is the key to success.

Trying to convince others that you are doing all this for self-fulfilment and not fame and fortune may cause some to roll their eyes and shake their heads. They don't understand that fame and fortune don't matter if you are not happy with yourself. Fame and fortune may help you with a few everyday comforts, but in the long run none of that matters if you aren't happy with yourself. Once you are happy with yourself, the money and success will follow. Those in the foothills cannot grasp this.

Decide what you truly want and you will be persistent. When you find what you should be doing, what really matters in your life, everything will come together to help you reach your goals.

If the want is big enough, the facts don't count. Also remember what Napoleon Hill said: 'There may be no heroic connotation to the word persistence, but the quality is to the character of human being, what carbon is to steel.'

Go and do it! Study success. Choose your want. And persist. Life will then be what it is meant to be!

IF YOU ARE HAVING TROUBLE WITH PERSISTENCE,

YOUR WANT IS PROBABLY PUNY. IT ISN'T BIG ENOUGH.

THAT IS PROBABLY THE CAUSE OF YOUR PROBLEM.

LOOK AROUND. IT IS A COMMON PROBLEM.

IT IS A HUMAN PROBLEM. LACK OF PERSISTENCE IS

ALMOST ALWAYS A SYMPTOM OF THE REAL PROBLEM.

YOU MUST GIVE THESE TWO CONCEPTS PRIORITY IN

YOUR LIFE: WANT AND PERSISTENCE.

Hang in There and Learn

Learn from your mistakes. Challenges will always be a part of your life. It is how you deal with the challenges, how you allow the obstacles to mould you into a better, stronger person that will decide if you become a success or a failure. What happens inside of you is what matters. The tougher you become mentally, the stronger you will be as a person.

The only place on earth that we know of where there are no problems is a cemetery. Everywhere else will be hit by the storms of life. If you remember that there is something to learn in every problem, then you can learn to grow by the storms rather than being crushed by them.

It's not what happens to us that counts; it's what happens
in us.

Instead of wishing that you never had to deal with the obstacles in your way, think how you can learn from them. It is only sheer ignorance and daydreaming to believe that you can live a life free of hardship and challenges. Every time you overcome a challenge you gain a tool to help you fight the next one. Life is a growing experience, and the only way to grow is to learn from the events that occur in life.

We go on experiencing life's lessons until we learn what we need to learn and then we can move on. Remember, above every stormy cloud is a bright sun which never fades.

There is something to learn in every adversity.

Hang in There and Find the Gem

There are two sides to every coin. One man's gloom is another man's glory. The Chinese call this the yin/yang principle. Every negative has a positive opposite. You just have to look for it. See your challenges in life as blessings in disguise, and try to uncover the hidden opportunities.

During the Great Depression, not everyone went belly-up. Some people actually became rich. When you see a problem, you also need to see an opportunity. One of the fastest ways to become wealthy is to solve someone else's problems or difficulties.

Many successful businesses today have been born out of someone's problem. Take the man who took surplus sawdust from the lumber mills free of charge and formulated several wood-burning products from it. He saw that lumberyards had a problem with excess sawdust. They didn't know what to do with it. He acted and began a wonderful business.

If it's going to be, it's up to me.

Hang in There and Be Patient

Every problem will go away. Either it will change or you will. No problem is permanent. It can't be permanent because everything is in a constant state of flux; everything changes. Worry is useless. Instead of being ready to give in, just remember that every problem has a limited lifespan. Things will get better. Seek to grow.

> *Tough times never last, but tough people do.*
>
> **–Robert Schuller**

How about Communism? Or the Berlin Wall? Who could have guessed that within days the entire Berlin Wall could be demolished? Within weeks, Communism would crumble. A problem which many people feared would plague the earth for centuries disappeared in a flash.

Look at your problem and ask will this matter in five years from now? What about next year?

Worry is like a rocking chair; it will give you something to do, but it won't get you anywhere.

Hang in There and Think

> THERE ARE NO PROBLEMS;
>
> THERE IS ONLY A SHORTAGE OF IDEAS.

Problems are not the problem. Ideas are the problem. Every problem, challenge or storm you face today has as its solution an idea waiting to be used. If you could only understand that the only thing standing between your current problem and the wiping away of it is nothing but an idea.

So, get your eyes off your problems and onto the solution. You may not be able to do anything about what has happened, but you surely can and should do something about finding a solution. That solution may seem like a fantasy right now, but keep in mind that the aeroplane was nothing but a fantasy until two brothers starting searching for ideas to solve their fantasy. Fantasies can become facts.

It was Christmas Eve. The large country church was filling up. The air was worshipful and festive. Families came from far and wide to enjoy the majestic organ playing the beautiful carols of the holidays.

But suddenly a problem arose. The service was about to begin when the organist discovered that a church mouse had chewed through the inner workings of the massive air chamber.

With only minutes to spare, the organist quickly composed a replacement carol which he played on his old acoustic guitar. The cords were simple and the melody sweet. That evening was the first time the world had ever heard the famous carol 'Silent Night.' By focusing on the solution instead of the problem, the result was spectacular.

Even the most successful people face challenges every day. In fact, they may face more challenges than the average person, and these challenges are probably very large. You are not alone in your struggles. And since you're not alone, why not align yourself with others who may be facing what you are facing? You could perhaps solve your problems together.

Chapter 13

Gratitude Is an Attractive Emotion

The man with no shoes grumbled in the street,
Until he met the man with no feet.

Many years ago there was a slave named Cato. One day Cato escaped from his master and fled to the forest. After many days of wondering without food or water, Cato stumbled upon a great tiger lying amongst the trees. Startled, Cato fled but soon realized that the tiger had not pursued him. He was curious why the giant tiger did not follow him and went back to investigate. As he approached the tiger, the great beast lifted its paw, and only then did Cato realize that it had been badly cut, as it was bloody and swollen.

Cato washed and bound the wound, and the great tiger licked the hand of Cato as a family dog might. The tiger took Cato to his cave and every day brought him meat to eat. Soon both man and tiger were strong and rejuvenated. But soon afterwards a search party found Cato and the tiger. The emperor sentenced Cato to be eaten by the same tiger he had befriended. People from around the kingdom came to witness the event.

The tiger was starved for many days so that it would be hungry and ruthless. Cato was placed in the centre of the arena so that all could see, and when the emperor commanded, a gate was raised and the tiger came running out, fierce and hungry.

It bore down on Cato like a multi-coloured bolt of lightning; but when it was just about to pounce, the tiger realized it was his old friend. The tiger calmed down and licked the hand of Cato while those in the audience watched in disbelief. The emperor, amazed at the spectacle, called on Cato, who told him the entire tale. Cato was then released and the tiger returned to his cave in the forest.

Gratitude is one of the most powerful emotions that a human being can possess. Researchers have discovered that people who are more grateful have higher levels of well-being. In general, they are happier, less depressed, less stressed and more satisfied with their lives and social relationships than those who take success for granted.

When you focus your thoughts and energy on all that is wrong in your life, you put yourself in a state of disharmony. You effectively resist all the wonderful things that could be occurring in your life. When this happens, you lower your vibrational energy level and ultimately attract more of what you don't want. As I have said many times before in this book, you attract whatever you think about. If you constantly think about why you won't or shouldn't get that promotion, then you will never receive the promotion.

Basically, you are being ungrateful for what you have at the moment. To think of it in another way, let's use this example. You take a child to an ice cream parlour after school one day so that she can have her favourite flavour. After receiving her scoop, she is ornery and just picks at the ice cream. She won't eat any unless she has two scoops. If she isn't happy with one scoop, why would you want to give her another? Now, if she had eaten the first scoop quickly while laughing and enjoying herself, you would see the joy that this scoop of ice cream gave the child. You would then want to purchase another scoop because you have seen the joy that it has brought to her life.

When you are grateful fear disappears
and abundance appears.

–Anthony Robbins

This attitude is applied to all aspects of your life. If your boss sees you constantly mourning because you think you are being held back or because you didn't get that promotion, he will never give it to you. But if you are happy and work with purpose and joy, he will see that as well and be more than happy to promote you. Your attitude rubs off on those around you. If you are grateful for your work and have a positive outlook, your boss will see that gratitude, and it will make him a happier person as well. We all want to be around those who make us feel good.

When good fortune enters your life, adopting an attitude of gratitude will connect your mind with the supreme source from which the blessings came, and you will be rewarded with even more gifts at an even faster pace.

I challenge you to begin looking for everything in your life you like and can appreciate. Once you see the benefits, you will want to live this way for the rest of your life.

Gratitude Exercise

Take three to five minutes throughout the day to give thanks to whoever or whatever you're grateful for. You don't have to do anything other than close your eyes and silently give thanks. This one act done regularly can make a huge difference. Remember gratitude brings love, health, happiness and prosperity. So be grateful and good things will find their way to you.

You've got one go in life, so make the most of it.

About the Author

Jorge Gannuny is an author, fitness specialist, professional speaker, photographer, filmmaker and philanthropist. When he was 19 years old, he accidentally came across a book that would propel him to share with people how to reach their full potential; a friend gave him a copy of The Power of Your Subconscious Mind by Dr Joseph Murphy. From that point, Jorge became obsessed with the human body and mind. He went on to study hundreds of books about psychology, fitness, philosophy, health, and beyond. Jorge now travels the globe learning and sharing his experience; he is constantly amazed with how powerful we are as human beings, and how intricately our mind works.

Website: jorgegannuny.com

Podcas: The Society of Greatness

thesocietyofgreatness.com

Notes

Notes

Printed in Poland
by Amazon Fulfillment
Poland Sp. z o.o., Wrocław

61819721R00083